the
Arts and Crafts
handbook

Hilary White

Step
forward
PUBLISHING

Acknowledgements

With grateful thanks to:

Ellie and Louise Dubuisson, William Freeman, Sarah Newbury, Eleanor Norris, Rachel, Michael and Jack Parker, Belle Walton, Joe and Hannah White

Julia Trew and children of Silverhill School, Winterbourne

The staff and children of the Maria Montessori School, Ealing

Cover Illustration

Clockwise, from top left:

Animal Paradise by Ellie Dubuisson, Robot by Joe White, Roller Ball Patterns by Sarah Newbury, Italian River by Joe White, Tortoise by William Freeman, Tartan Lady by Rachel Parker, Blue Butterfly by Hannah White

Published by Step Forward Publishing Limited
St Jude's Church, Dulwich Road, Herne Hill, London, SE24 0PB
Tel: 020 7738 5454 www.practicalpreschool.com

Production and Design by Alison Cutler, Fonthill Creative 01722 716996

Printed in UK by Ashford Colour Press Limited

ISBN: 978 1 90 4575 06 1

Contents

Introduction

About this book

Everyone who enjoys doing art and craft with children will find inspiration in this comprehensive art and craft handbook. It offers a wealth of arty ideas for parents, childminders, early years workers, teachers and out-of-school club leaders.

If you want to try papier mâché but can't remember the recipe ... if you are not sure what to do with plaster of Paris ... if you want some tips on using glass paint ... this is the book for you! Use it to trigger your children's creativity and help them discover the pleasures of art and craft. You will be amazed at just how much they can do with pencils, paint, clay and all the many other materials that can be turned into stunning artwork.

How do I find my way around?

The activities are organised by the type of materials used. If you want to use up all that silver foil in the back of the cupboard, or you want to try out some different ways of using tissue paper, simply turn to the appropriate chapter in the book. The chapters are as follows:

- Pencils
- Paint
- Wax crayons, chalk and pastels
- Card, textured paper and papercraft
- Tissue paper, cellophane and silver foil
- Newspaper, magazines, wrapping paper and greetings cards
- Beans and pasta, flowers and leaves
- Fabric and buttons, wool and string
- Sand and shells, stone, wood and glass
- Clay, plaster of Paris and other modelling materials

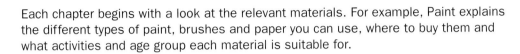

Each chapter begins with a look at the relevant materials. For example, Paint explains the different types of paint, brushes and paper you can use, where to buy them and what activities and age group each material is suitable for.

What will I find?

Most of the activities in the book focus on the basic skills of art and craft such as how to use a paint brush to create different effects; how to roll a ball of clay; different ways of folding, tearing and cutting paper to create textures and patterns. Once children have these and other techniques at their finger tips, they can draw on their storehouse of skills to produce their own creative artwork.

If you want some specific pointers for using a skill or technique, there is also a Use For section attached to the activities. This gives lots of ideas for turning a particular activity into a piece of art. For example, the basic technique of spraying paint can be used to make a textured beach scene or a stencilled pattern for wrapping paper. The basic techniques of folding and cutting paper can be used to make fans, Chinese lanterns, Christmas garlands and paper lace window decorations.

How do I find ideas for my art and craft project?

The index at the back of the book lists the key pieces of art you can make using the activities described in the book. Where relevant, they are grouped into themes and topics, so if you want to do an art and craft project linked to food or animals, you will find a list of ideas under F or A respectively. If you want to make a card or present for Mother's Day, check in the index for lists of ideas.

How do I choose what to do?

Each activity has a minimum age attached to its title. When it comes to art and craft, any age recommendations should be regarded as fluid. Different children develop at very different rates, and their capabilities depend partly on their previous experience. You also need to take into account how much adult help the children will have. Although it is important not to interfere too much with a child's work, you can afford to be a bit more ambitious if you are working with just a couple of children, rather than a class of 30!

Pick and choose activities to suit the interests, needs, age and skill base of your children. With such a large collection of activities, you will be able to find something for everyone. If you have children who need to be on the move, get them making a large, Jackson Pollock-style 'action painting'. If you have children who enjoy intricate work, set them the challenge of creating a detailed collage with beans and pulses or ribbons, lace and beads. If you are painting with babies, check out Finger painting or Painting with the under 4s. If you are painting with arty eight year olds, have a look at some techniques for using water colours - for example Wet paper and watery paint.

What do I do with finished art?

Once children have completed a piece of artwork, show it off with a beautiful mount. Choose colours that complement the picture and experiment with double and triple mounts, different shaped mounts and border widths. You can also decorate the borders of a mount with patterns such as prints or wax engravings. The pictures in this book have been mounted in a variety of different ways. If you need a few ideas, use them for inspiration. You can also get older children to come up with their own ideas and techniques.

Chapter 1

Pencils

About Pencils

Pencils come in lots of different shapes and sizes. For little children, the chunkier, hexagonal ones are easier to grip than smooth-sided pencils. You can also get triangular shaped pencils. These encourage children to hold the pencil in the correct manner - although an unusual grip is not a problem unless it is hampering the child's drawing.

The standard pencil grade is HB, which is ideal for writing. Softer drawing pencils are graded from B upwards (B, 2B, 3B and so on). The higher the number, the softer and smudgier the line. The softest grade that can easily be purchased from stationers is 7B. For a hard pencil, look out for an H, 2H and so on. The H grades give a hard, light line. They don't need sharpening as often as the B grade pencil but they are not so easy to draw with.

Apart from the traditional wood encased graphite pencil, you can also get pure graphite sticks. These give much the same results as a standard pencil, but they have a different weight and feel. Offer them to young artists who are taking their drawing seriously and enjoy exploring new implements.

Coloured pencils can also be chubby, standard sized, smooth-sided or triangular. Look out for the water soluble variety. These can be used as ordinary coloured pencils or washed with a paint brush and water to produce a watery effect. Coloured pencils are quite subtle compared with paint, wax crayons or felt pens. Invest in the best that you can afford. A child's drawing experience will be considerably more satisfying if the quality of the materials is good.

Look out for metallic effect pencils and a skin tone selection, with shades to reflect the different complexions of a multi-racial society. For something a little different, try rainbow pencils. These have a lead made up of different coloured stripes. Try using metallic, rainbow and lighter coloured pencils such as white and yellow on dark paper.

Charcoal can be used in similar ways to a soft pencil, except that it is even softer and tends to give a thicker, darker line. It also breaks easily. Save it until children are at least eight when they can control its smudginess. Show them how to hold the stick near

the drawing point, to prevent it from snapping, and make sure there's soap and water nearby for washing blackened fingers! You can also buy charcoal pencils, which give you the effect of charcoal without creating quite so much mess.

About drawing paper

Any paper can be used for drawing, although certain types work better for different drawing materials. Keep a supply of smooth, white cartridge paper for special drawings. Cartridge paper is a little more expensive than sugar or all-purpose papers but it is satisfying to work on and it shows the children that their drawings are valued. Offer different coloured papers as well as white, and encourage the children to think about which colour to choose. A buff, light grey or pale green background can make quite a difference to a pencil drawing, particularly if you are using a soft, dark pencil. Brightly coloured and black papers are also fun to explore, particularly with metallic or light coloured pencils.

About erasers

There is no place for an eraser in children's art, unless you are using it to create an effect (*see Pencil effects/Eraser drawing, page 12*). Pre-school children won't think of using a rubber if it isn't suggested to them. Older children are often more self-critical about their art work, and it can be harder to dissuade them from trying to rub out their drawings. If they insist on having an eraser to hand, keep reminding them that lightly drawn pencil rubs out more easily than heavy lines.

Why draw with pencils?

- Pencils are cheap, accessible and easy for even the youngest artists to handle. Young children need lots of opportunity for mark-making as part of their development as artists and writers – and pencils are an essential part of this experience.
- As children get older, they become more able to make choices about what to put in a drawing and how to use drawing tools. Once they have been shown a few of the possibilities, they can go on to create all kinds of different effects with a pencil.
- The pencil is an exact drawing tool. More than any other medium, it enables the children to produce precision, detail and shading in their art work. Pencils are ideal for exploring the art elements of 'line' and 'outline'.

Activities

Free drawing (all ages)

As soon as children are able to hold a pencil they can start to draw, although most children do not produce pictures 'of something' until they are about three and a half. This early, pre-representational stage is important. Encourage children to explore pencils and paper as much as possible and value their early drawings, even if they appear to be just scribbles. Watch out for the moment at which those random scribbles develop into controlled lines and enclosed shapes – and then into people, animals, houses and vehicles ...

You will need

- Pencils, ranging from HB to 2B
- White cartridge paper
- Different coloured papers

What to do

Make drawing materials constantly available to children and encourage them to draw whenever they want. Sit down yourself and draw with young children, whether you are at home, at school or in a play setting. They can watch how you hold and manipulate the pencil and it introduces the idea that a drawing can be 'of something'. Try drawing a shape for them to turn into their own picture. What will they do with a circle, a square, a triangle or a trapezium?

Observational drawing (4+)

Once children have realised that a picture can be 'of something', introduce looking closely at an object and drawing what you see. This is a skill that is central to art, whether the subject matter is a still life (a group of inanimate objects), life drawing (people), portraits, landscapes or nature drawings.

You will need

- Pencils, ranging from HB to 2B
- White cartridge paper
- Different coloured papers (optional)
- Objects to draw (*see WHAT TO DRAW box, page 10*)

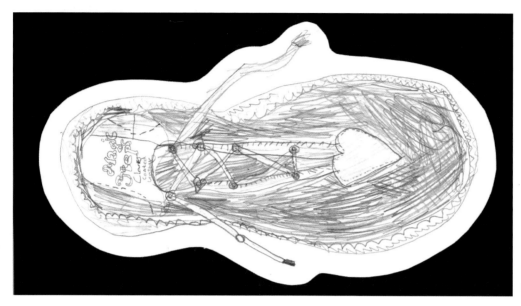

My Shoe by Hannah (6)

What to do

Choose an object to suit the purpose; for example, if children are just starting to make observational drawings, go for items with simple shapes such as a hyacinth bulb in a glass bulb jar. If you want to draw attention to lines and details with older children, choose something more complex such as a shell or an intricate flower. Wherever possible, try to find something to match specific interests – a toy truck for the car mad child or a model horse for an animal lover.

Look at the item with the children. Identify the different shapes and patterns – for example, the circles that make up the wheels of a car, the squares and rectangles that make up the doors and windows of a house, the pattern of veins on a leaf. They will enjoy using a magnifying glass to study small details.

Introduce the drawing materials and paper to the children. Emphasise that the white cartridge paper is for special drawings. Offer a range of coloured papers to choose from and encourage children to think about their subject matter – a light green for a nature drawing, pale pink for delicate shells, bright red for a robust drawing of a fire engine. As the children draw, remind them to keep on looking at the object.

If children know how to use the pencil to create some different effects (*see Pencil effects, page 11*), talk about whether they want to add dots, cross hatching or other features to their drawing.

What to draw

- Objects with an interesting pattern of lines such as shells, shoes, stringed instruments.
- Items (with a distinctive shape, such as flowers and leaves).
- Favourite things, such as model cars or animals.
- Objects that relate to a particular theme, for example clothes, toys, food.

Pencil effects (3.5+)

Once children discover that they can create lots of different effects with a pencil, it adds a whole new dimension to their drawings. Many of the following techniques are so simple that even very young children can have a go.

You will need

- Pencils in a range of different grades
- White cartridge paper
- A good eraser
- A pencil sharpener

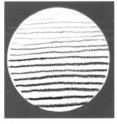

Different pressures

Different pressures (3.5+): show the children how to press gently to make a light mark, and harder to produce a dark mark. Challenge older children to create a series of shades from light to dark. Experiment with different grades of pencil.

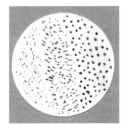

Making dots

Making dots (3.5+): show the children how to make dots with the pencil. This can range from the three year old simply stabbing with a soft, blunt pencil to the five plus age group drawing tiny controlled circles.

Smudging

Smudging (3.5+): draw lines and zig-zags with a soft pencil (at least 2B if not softer). Show the children how to smudge the pencil markings with a finger.

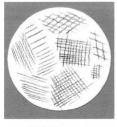

Hatching and
cross hatching

Hatching and cross hatching (4.5+): hatching consists of drawing lots of pencil lines close together. To turn hatching into cross hatching, draw a second set of lines crossing the first. Experiment with different pressures to create dark and light shades. Try cross hatching with slanted lines. Cross light lines with dark lines, using either different pressures or a hard pencil (H grade) teamed with a soft pencil (B grade).

What to do

Using the side of the pencil (5+): sharpen a soft pencil so that it has a long point. Show the children how to hold the pencil so that they can draw a thick smudgy line with the side of the point.

More details: draw zig-zags, curved lines, wavy lines, loops and any other patterns. Try drawing zig-zags and wavy lines close together.

Eraser drawing (5+): run the side of a soft, sharp pencil over a sheet of paper and smudge with a finger. Holding the paper firmly, use an eraser to make white markings in the smudgy black pencil.

What other pencil effects can you and your children come up with? Give the children lots of opportunity to play with the different pencil effects and encourage them to use the techniques in other drawings.

Use for

Pencil effects in free drawing: choose some books to look at with the children and point out drawings which use different techniques such as cross hatching, dots and darker and lighter areas. For example, John Burningham uses cross hatching in his picture book *Mr Gumpy's Outing*. Get the children thinking about which techniques to use for a particular type of drawing or subject matter. *See USING PENCIL EFFECTS box opposite for some suggestions.*

Patchwork Pencil Pattern by Leah (11)

Patchwork pencil patterns: draw a grid of squares using a pencil and ruler. Make a patchwork pattern by filling in each square with a different pencil effect. Patchwork pencil patterns can be used for anything that needs decorating – work folders, book covers, wrapping paper, paper to cover boxes, wallpaper for doll's houses, large picture frames and mounts.

Using pencil effects

Try different drawing techniques to create particular effects:

- Shading with the side of the pencil point is good for adding interest to big items such as trees, houses and mountains.
- Dots and cross hatching can be used to add texture to drawings of houses and landscapes.
- Dots and hatching add detail to drawings of animals, birds and plants.
- Smudging is effective for drawings of clouds, water and shadows.
- Use eraser drawings to make clouds, patterns on water and aeroplane vapour trails.

Drawing with coloured pencils (all ages)

You will need

- Coloured pencils
- White cartridge paper / different coloured papers
- A pencil sharpener

What to do

Allow children to use coloured pencils freely. As they learn how to cross hatch, shade with the side of the pencil and make dots, remind them that they can try out these effects with coloured pencils, as well as ordinary pencils. Try the following:

Coloured dots (5+): make dots using two different colours such as yellow and red. Look at the dots from a distance. What colour can you see?

Cross hatching: use two different colours to make cross hatch patterns.

Blending colours: colour in an area of the paper. Colour over the top with a different colour. Always use the lighter colour second and press lightly with the darker colour. For example, a gentle pressure for an area of blue followed by a harder pressure for yellow.

Blending lines of colour: use the same technique as blending colours, above, except that you use the side of a sharpened pencil point to create lines of colour.

Use for

Nature drawings: the soft, subtle quality of coloured pencils makes them really good for drawings of plants, flowers, trees and wildlife. Try drawing a plant using greens, browns and greys on beige, cream or pale green paper.

Greetings cards with the under threes: even the earliest drawings can be turned into a greetings card. Choose coloured paper and a selection of coloured pencils to

complement the colour of the background paper. Cut the paper into an interesting shape such as a circle, a long thin strip, a star or a heart. Let the child draw freely on the paper and then mount the drawing onto folded card. Use star shaped paper for a Christmas card, or a heart shape for Valentine's Day. Drawing with felt pens will give a stronger, brighter drawing, although very young children will need careful supervision.

A limited colour palette: try limiting children to just two or three coloured pencils and ask them to add a small amount of colour to a pencil drawing. Adding just a few small coloured details can also make an attractive Christmas card. Draw holly and a robin or a decorated Christmas tree with a dark pencil or a thin black felt pen. Colour in the robin's breast and the holly berries with red. Colour in just a few of the baubles and the star at the top of the Christmas tree with yellow, orange and red. This technique also works well with coloured felt-tipped pens, particularly if you use gold and silver pens for stars and baubles.

Pointillist drawings: Seurat and Signac were two 19th Century French artists who used tiny dots of paint to create their paintings. Try making your own pointillist pictures using coloured pencil dots (*see also Brush effects / Pointillist paintings, page 25*).

Colourful patchwork patterns: draw a grid of squares using a pencil and ruler and ask the children to fill in each square with a different coloured pencil effect (*see also Pencil effects / Patchwork pencil patterns, page 12*).

Shaded drawings (6+)

Older children can start to look at the patterns of light and shadow on an item, and then use their pencil to depict the shading on their drawing. This is the first step towards making a drawing appear three dimensional.

You will need

- Pencils in a range of different grades
- White cartridge paper
- A pencil sharpener

What to do

Choose an item that clearly shows shadows and reflected light. Glazed white pottery or plain wooden sculptures usually work well. Encourage the children to look out for shadows and reflected light on the surface of the object. Show them how to use small zig-zags to create the shaded areas on their drawings. More experienced artists can try shading with cross hatching, dots and using the side of the pencil.

Where to draw

Explore different parts of the home or setting to find a place where the lighting clearly shows up the contrast between the light and shadow on the object. If possible, do your shaded drawing in this spot.

Chapter 2

Paint

About paint

When it comes to choosing paint, there are endless possibilities. The most commonly used children's paints are 'ready mixed' and powder paint. Ready mixed paint is convenient, it comes in bottles and can be squeezed directly into a paint pot. If you want to experiment with different thicknesses you can thin it down with water. Look out for bright fluorescent colours such as lime green and electric blue; pearlescent pastel colours and metallic colours such as gold, silver and copper. Powder paint has to be mixed with water, although you can create some interesting effects by sprinkling it directly onto wet paper (*see Wet paper and watery paint / Sprinkling powder paint, page 34*). You can control the thickness of the powder paint by the amount of water you add.

Finger paints are another option, particularly for very young children. Although it is possible to finger paint with ready mixed or powder paint (*see Finger painting, page 18*), specialised finger paint has a thick, glossy texture which makes it particularly satisfying to use.

Acrylic paints are suitable for the seven plus age group. They come in tubes or bottles and they have a slightly plastic quality that creates texture in your painting. Like oil paints they can be smeared directly onto the paper with a palette knife and they will also retain the brush marks if you use them thickly. At the same time, you can water them down and use them like water colours. They are waterproof when dry.

Water colours can also be introduced to the seven plus age group. They come in tubes or solid blocks (called pans). Both types need to be mixed with water prior to use, although the pans tend to be more economical than the tubes. Water colours give clear, vibrant colours and they are particularly good for delicate work, colour washes and paintings of sky or water.

Apart from standard paints, there are a number of specialist paints available for working on different surfaces. These include fabric paints, glass paints (*see Glass painting, page 155*) and marbling inks for making marbled patterns on paper (*see Marbling, page 39*).

About paper for painting

Any paper can be used for painting, but you do need to choose a paper to suit the paint you are using, or the effect you want to create. Heavy paints such as acrylics or thick powder paint need sugar paper or cartridge paper. Use stiff card for activities where the paint has been given extra body with flour (*see Pasty paint, page 37*) or PVA glue (*see PVA paint, page 38*). Watery paintings (*see page 34*) also work best on a tough paper such as specialised watercolour paper. Most watercolour paper is as heavy as stiff card and it has a slightly stippled surface. It is more expensive than sugar or even cartridge paper, but the textured surface adds an attractive quality to the paint. The robustness of watercolour paper also means that it can take even the thinnest paint without crinkling when dry.

Offer children different coloured papers, including dark ones such as black and dark blue, to paint on and encourage them to think about which colour to choose for their picture. Metallic, pearlescent and fluorescent paints show up particularly well on darker backgrounds. Have fun exploring – how about lime green paint on orange paper, or turquoise on pink?

About brushes

For very little children, choose brushes with chunky handles and thick bristles. It is also useful to provide brushes with coloured handles to remind children which paint pot the brush should be returned to. With older children, try to choose an appropriate brush for a particular activity, for more delicate paintings children can experiment with thinner brushes.

The two main brush shapes are 'flat ended' and 'round'. The flat ended brush will give you a nice wide brush stroke and is good for large acrylic paintings. The rounded brush can be shaped into a point with the fingers so that you can achieve fine lines and dots. You could also look out for brushes with a slanted edge, soft fan shaped brushes, traditional Chinese calligraphy brushes and stencil brushes, which have short, hard wearing bristles. For splattering and flicking paint, and painting large areas, you can also use decorating brushes.

About other paint tools

As well as brushes, try exploring with pieces of sponge, paper towels or feathers. Thick paints such as acrylics can be smeared directly onto paper with a plastic kitchen spatula or bendy palette knife. Cotton buds are another versatile resource – great for those occasions when you want very little children to dab paint onto a small area, without mixing up the colours (*for example, Painting pebbles, page 148*). They can also be used for smudging and stippling thick ready mixed and acrylic paints, or lifting wet water colours off the paper (*see Wet paper and watery paint / Lifting off wet paint, page 35*). You can also purchase specialised paint tools, including shaped sponges with handles, patterned paint rollers and combs for making patterns in textured paint.

Paint

About paint accessories

Apart from the paint, the brushes and the paper, you will need a place for children to work, containers to hold the paint, and a mixing palette for children who are starting to blend colours and make different shades.

A free-standing easel is super for younger children, allowing them to paint standing up and see clearly what they are doing. For the serious older artist who enjoys painting at home, a table top easel is cheaper and doesn't take up so much space. If children are working on flat table tops invest in a piece of pvc fabric – it's a wipeable surface protector that can be used time and again.

For ready mixed or powder paint, get some non-spill paint pots. These have special lids with small holes for the brush so that the paint doesn't spill if they are knocked over. If possible, choose pots with coloured lids to match the colour of the paint. Look out for pots with rubber bungs or air tight lids. This will stop the paint drying up when not in use.

Once children have started to explore colour mixing, you will need a mixing palette (*see Colour mixing, page 23*). White palettes with separate sections are cheap but a plain white plate will do just as well. For acrylics and water colours, you will also need a water jar.

Why paint?

- You can give paint body and texture by adding substances such as flour or sand.
- You can create bright, bold pictures with finger paint or thick powder paint.
- You can mix up watery paint solutions and work on finely textured paper to create delicate, subtle effects.
- You can spray it, flick it, dribble it or use it for printing.

Paint is suitable for all ages. Even toddlers can dab away with a chunky brush, whereas older children can produce a fine degree of detail with thin brushes and watercolour paints.

Compared with pencils, paint is a very 'obvious' medium. Young children can immediately see the results of their activities on the paper. This helps them to discover that they can change the appearance of the paper by making marks – an important element of becoming an artist.

Paint is the best way to explore colour:

- Most paints produce vibrant colours that stand out against a background, particularly if the child is working on white paper.
- New colours can be created by mixing together two or more colours.
- You can change the shade or tone of a colour by adding white or black, or changing the ratio of one colour to another in a colour mix.
- You can change the qualities of a colour by adding more pigment or more water to a paint mix.

For more on manipulating paint to create different tones and shades, see Colour mixing *(page 23)*.

Paint is an immensely satisfying medium to use. If children are given the space and freedom to enjoy painting, it can be a very therapeutic and calming activity.

Activities

Finger painting (all ages)

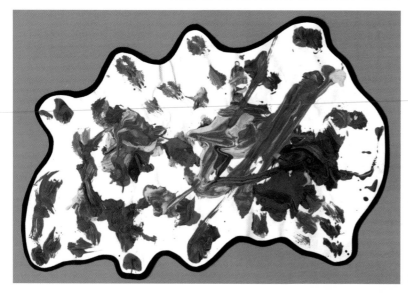

Finger Painting by Belle (3)

Finger painting is a good way to introduce very young children to the textures and quality of paint - many older children enjoy it too!

You will need

• Finger paint
• Shallow containers for the paint
• A large sheet of sturdy paper or card

What to do

Place the different coloured paints in shallow containers. Show the children how to scoop out handfuls of paint and place them on the paper. Encourage them to explore the paint:

• make handprints
• make fingerprints
• make lines with their fingers

- make swirly patterns
- blend the colours with a finger to create a streaky effect
- mix together two colours to create a new colour

You can also finger paint with ready mixed paint or a thick mixture of powder paint. Try mixing paint with flour or cornflour for a stiffer texture. Compare the feel of the different paints. Which do the children prefer?

Tip

Finger painting is a classic 'messy play' activity. Work next to hand-washing facilities or have soap, towel and a bowl of warm water nearby. If younger children do not want to get their hands painty, let them join in with a handled sponge brush.

Painting with the under 4s

Flowers by Maanya (4)

Children of this age group should be left free to enjoy the paint and discover its many visual and tactile qualities. As a starting point, show them how to manage the practicalities of painting so that they can use the painting materials as independently as possible.

You will need

- Ready mixed or powder paint, in non-spill pots
- A brush for each pot, preferably with a handle to match the colour of the paint
- A free standing easel with a shelf to hold the paint pots
- A supply of painting paper
- An apron
- A plastic floor mat
- Space for leaving wet paintings to dry, such as a clear floor, clothes rack or clothes line with pegs

What to do

If you are painting with children younger than three, you will need to prepare the painting materials and supervise closely. The three plus age group can be shown how to organise the painting materials for themselves. These practical little tasks will vary, depending on whether you are painting at home or in an early years setting, but they will probably include some or all of the following:

• Putting on an apron
• Where to find the painting paper
• Attaching the paper to the easel
• Putting the paint brush back in the right pot
• How to wipe the brush on the side of the pot's opening so the bristles are not overloaded with paint
• Where to put the painting to dry
• Washing hands

Once the children can get themselves going, leave them to explore the paint freely. Encourage them to talk about their paintings, but avoid asking direct questions such as 'what is it?' Many children don't do representational paintings until they are three and a half and the question will simply confuse them. Look out for the moment when a child starts to tell you what their picture shows. This indicates they realise that pictures can represent the world around them – an important conceptual milestone!

For children younger than four, start off with just two or three primary colours (red, yellow, blue). Add other colours as they become more able to cope with the paint pots and brushes. Avoid black unless you want to create a particular effect, as it can drown other colours.

Watch the children at work and when you feel they are ready to explore some new painting possibilities, try introducing some of the skills and activities in this section.

Line, area and space (3+)

In the early stages of painting, young children tend to dab at the paper and explore the paint in what appears to be a random way. Gradually, they will start to produce controlled lines and shapes and make decisions about which parts of the paper to paint and which to leave blank. If you feel a child is ready, try introducing some little activities to highlight the art elements of 'line', 'area' and 'space'.

You will need

• Painting paper
• Ready mixed / powder paints
• Thick and thin brushes
• Cotton buds
• A free standing easel
• Thin card, scissors and blu-tack
• A selection of tartan and other fabrics with a pattern of lines

Paint

What to do

Painted Lines by William (11)

Painting lines: highlight 'line' as a feature of painting by giving children some starting points for exploring painted lines. Work on white paper and choose a strongly coloured paint such as red. Paint a straight line across the centre of the paper. Challenge the children to paint a line from the top of the paper to the bottom, and from one side to the other. Paint different types of line: a wiggly line, a zig-zag, a curved line, a long line, a short line. Observe how the line becomes fainter as the paint on the brush is used up. Experiment with different sized brushes to produce thin lines and thick lines. Try wiping across a thick line of paint with a cotton bud, to create smudgy train tracks. Older children with good brush control can try decorating thick lines and painting criss-cross patterns. Have a look at some tartan patterns and checked fabrics for ideas and inspiration.

Painting areas: introduce some techniques for painting a solid area of colour. Paint the outline of a shape and fill it in with lines of paint. Can the children keep within the outline and not leave any of the paper showing? As with painting lines, experiment with thick and thin brushes, faint and strong lines and different colours. Find other ways of filling in solid areas – sponge painting, stippling with a thick brush (*see Brush effects / Stippling, page 26*) or using a wide decorating brush.

Leaving spaces: focus on the option of leaving some parts of the paper unpainted. Look at a painting and point out the difference between the painted areas and the blank areas. Use masking tape to help the children create blank spaces in their paintings. The tape can either be torn into pieces or cut into shapes (*see MAKING STENCILS box, page 22*). Stick the masking tape onto the paper and paint across it. When the paint is dry, peel off the tape to reveal the blank spaces beneath. Experiment with contrasting colours (such as pale yellow paper and bright red paint) and shades of the same colour (such as dark green paper and pale green paint).

Use for

Decorative papers: painted tartans and patterns of lines can be used for decorating work folders, book covers, mounts for pictures, wallpaper for doll's houses and wrapping paper. They can also be used to make collage clothes for cut-out people.

Easter cards: cut out a large egg shape from a sheet of folded card. Open out the card and ask the children to decorate the front and the back with lines of paint and other brush effects (*see page 26*). Decorate the front of the card with a cellophane bow.

Hallowe'en pumpkin: masking tape stencils can be used for any project that needs clear, distinctive shapes. To make a Hallowe'en pumpkin, cut out a pumpkin shape from

black paper. Cut out eyes, nose and mouth stencils from masking tape and greaseproof paper, stick them onto the pumpkin and paint with orange paint. When the paint is dry, peel off the stencils to reveal the features beneath.

Tartan Lady by Rachel (11)

Making stencils

To make masking tape stencils, stick a strip of masking tape onto greaseproof paper. Draw simple shapes on the tape and cut them out, leaving a tab of greaseproof paper at the side of the shape. Carefully peel the shapes off the greaseproof paper and stick them onto a sheet of paper, ready for painting. Go for simple shapes such as triangles, rectangles and circles – more complicated shapes tend to tear as you peel them off the greaseproof paper.

Using masking fluid

Children older than seven who have had some experience of water colours can also be introduced to masking fluid. Paint the masking fluid onto watercolour paper with an ordinary brush – it will dry to form a thin rubbery skin that protects the underlying paper. Paint over the paper and masking fluid. Once the paint is dry, rub off the masking fluid with a finger to reveal the blank spaces beneath.

Colour mixing (4+)

Once children can mix colours, they can use a huge range of different shades and tones in their painting. Often, they will discover colour mixing for themselves, through finger painting or accidentally mixing the colours on the painting paper. You can then introduce other colour mixing possibilities.

You will need

- Red, blue and yellow paint – ready mixed, powder paint or, for older ones, acrylics or watercolours
- Brushes, with handles to match each colour, plus a 'mixing brush' with a plain wooden handle.
- Water (for older children)
- Mixing palette or white plate
- White cartridge paper

What to do

Choose two primary colours, such as yellow and red. Put a blob of red and a blob of yellow on the mixing palette. Using the special 'mixing brush', blend the two colours to make orange. Identify the new colour and show how the shade of orange changes when you add more yellow or more red. Emphasise the importance of using the mixing brush to mix, and not getting red paint on the yellow brush or vice versa. Make other secondary colours by mixing together two primaries:

- red + blue = purple
- yellow + blue = green
- yellow + red = orange

Once children are ready to mix lots of colours in one painting session, provide them with a jar of water. Show them how to rinse their brush before going on to the next colour. Emphasise the importance of changing the water regularly.

As children become more experienced with colour mixing, introduce them to different colour mixing possibilities:

- Add white to lighten colours.
- Add a tiny amount of black to darken colours.
- Change the shade of a secondary colour (purple, green, orange) by adjusting the ratio of the primary colours in the mix – less yellow and more blue makes a dark, oily green, more yellow and less blue makes a paler green.
- Mix black and white to make grey.
- Mix red and white to make pink.
- Mix all three primary colours (red, yellow, blue) to make brown.
- Make different browns by mixing two secondary colours; compare a brown mixed from green and purple with a brown mixed from green and orange.
- Explore the link between saturation and shade. Saturation refers to the density of a colour, so a thick powder paint has a high saturation, whereas a thin water colour has a low saturation. Compare how saturation affects the shade of the colour.

Tip
The process of colour mixing can be quite complicated. Give support to children who are not ready to organise all the different paints, palettes and brushes by themselves.

Use for

Shaded paintings: once children can mix different shades of colour, they can use a range of shades to add interest to their pictures. For example, a sandy beach painted in shades of yellow, ochre and light brown, or a tree using lots of greens and browns.

Shaded stripes: put a large blob of white on a mixing palette. Add a small amount of colour to the white and mix thoroughly to make a pale shade. Paint a stripe across the top of the paper. Add a bit more colour to make a slightly darker shade and paint another stripe, just beneath the first. Continue painting darker and darker stripes. The final stripe should be just the colour, with no added white. Next try darkening a colour with black, adding tiny quantities of black to the original colour. The shaded stripes can be cut into shapes – balloons, candy sticks (to stick on Christmas trees), legs wearing stripy tights (for a collage person) or a stripy marmalade cat.

Getting good colour mixes

The three primary colours of red, blue and yellow come in different shades, and some make better colour mixes than others. If you are ordering paint from a schools supplier, ask their advice over which colours to choose for colour mixing. The following is a rough guide:

- Ultramarine blue and crimson make a good purple
  (otherwise, not an easy colour to mix).
- Lemon yellow and cobalt or Prussian blue make a good green.
- Vermillion red can be mixed with any yellow to make orange.
- Yellow ochre is good for adding to red to make earthy colours.

People painting (3.5+)

Skin colours come in a huge variety of different tones and shades. People painting offers some great colour mixing opportunities for older children, as well as the chance to explore the variety in the human race. For younger children, you can buy sets of ready mixed skin tone paints.

You will need

- Set of ready mixed skin tone paints (for younger children)
- Mixing brushes, palette and ready mixed or acrylic paints in red, blue, yellow, white and black (for 7+ age group)

- White cartridge paper
- Pictures or photographs of people with different skin tones

What to do

Look at the pictures with the children. With younger ones, choose a skin tone paint that matches the complexion of the person in the picture. For older children, cut out the picture and blu-tack it to some scrap paper. Mix up a skin tone and brush it next to the picture. Decide whether or not the shade matches the person's skin tone and adjust the colour if necessary. To mix up skin tones, try the following:

- Start off by blending white and red to make pink.
- Add a little yellow to make the pink more flesh toned.
- For darker complexions, add blue or even a little black.
- Adjust the red, yellow and white in the mix, as necessary.

Once the children have the right colours, they can go ahead with painting their pictures. Encourage younger ones to paint in the face, rather than just painting an outline for the head. Cut out eyes, nose and mouth from masking tape and stick them onto the face before filling it in (see Line, area and space / Painting areas, page 21). The blank features can then be painted on, once the face is dry.

Use for

A portrait garden: paint family, friends or school group. The children can sit for portrait painting sessions or gather photographs of family and friends. Mount each face in the centre of a large cut-out flower, with stalk and leaves. Attach the portrait flowers to a 'garden' background, made from sponge painted soil and cut-out blades of green grass.

A friendship frieze: cut out a chain of paper people and paint their faces with different people paint (see Paper cutting / Paper chains, page 78).

Brush effects (3.5+)

A paint brush can be a surprisingly versatile tool. Try using it in different ways to create a variety of interesting effects.

You will need

- Several paint brushes, including a brush with long, soft bristles, a flat ended brush, a round brush with a point, and a thick bristled brush
- Ready mixed, powder paint, acrylics and water colours
- White cartridge paper
- Different coloured papers

What to do

Introduce the following techniques:

Stippling

Stippling (3+): load a thick bristled brush with ready mixed or powder paint and stab it against the paper to create a stippled effect. Watch how the stippling changes as the paint gets used up. Encourage older children to vary the force of their stabbing to create different effects. Save old brushes for this activity, as the bristles will get damaged!

Brush strokes

Brush strokes (3+): make brush strokes using a brush loaded with ready mixed, powder or acrylic paint. Look at how the bristles create a texture in the thick paint, particularly if you are using acrylics. Observe how the appearance of the brush stroke changes, as the brush gets drier and drier.

Fans

Fans (4+): using a brush with long, soft bristles, load the brush with ready mixed, powder or acrylic paint and then press the brush flat against the paper to create a 'fan' effect. Observe how the fans change as the paint gets used up.

Dots

Dots (7+): using a round brush, dampen the brush with water and stroke the tip of the bristles into a point. Dip the pointed tip into paint and make small dots.

Rectangles (7+): using a flat ended brush, dip the end of the brush in paint and gently pull it across the paper. Create long strips of colour, or a row of small squares or rectangles. Experiment with thick paint or thin water colours.

What other brush effects can you and your children come up with?

Use for

Stencilling: cut out card shapes or cut a shape out of a piece of thin card to make a stencil. Attach the shapes or the stencil to the paper with tiny blobs of blu-tak and stipple over them to create stencilled patterns. Use for making greetings cards, gift tags and wrapping paper.

Animals: use a fairly dry brush to make strokes of paint for hair and animal fur. Dots, fans and stippling make effective animal markings.

Buildings: using a flat ended brush, paint separate rectangles to make the bricks and tiles for houses.

Pointillist paintings: Seurat and Signac were two 19th Century French artists who used tiny dots of colour to create their paintings. Try making your own pointillist paintings using the tip of a pointed paint brush. If your children run out of patience, you can also create a pointillist effect by spraying paint onto the paper (*see Spraying paint, page 28*).

Dribbling and flicking paint (all ages)

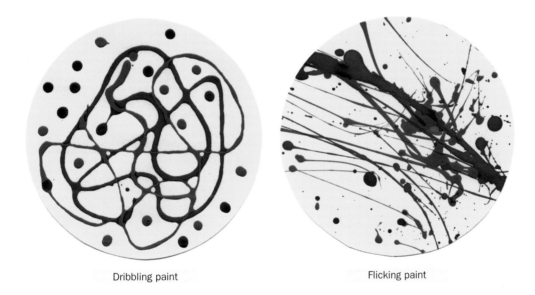

Dribbling paint   Flicking paint

Dribbling paint directly from the bottle and flicking it from a large brush are fun ways to enjoy paint. Minimise the mess by using a large piece of paper and, if possible, work outdoors or in a garage.

You will need

• Ready mixed paint in squeezy bottles
• Large brushes, including decorator's brushes
• Large strips of paper, such as the back of un-pasted wallpaper

What to do

Check that the paint dribbles easily from the bottles. If you are painting with a group, make sure that each child has their own area of paper to work on. Show the children how to dribble paint directly from the bottle onto the paper. As they get the hang of it, encourage them to try the following:

Lines: move the bottle along to create lines. Try making thick lines by moving the bottle slowly, and thin lines by moving it quickly.

Shapes: experiment with making wavy lines, zig-zags, loops and different shapes.

Blobs and splashes: stand over the painting and drip the paint from a height, to create blobs and splashes. What happens if you drop the paint from different heights?

Combining colours: make a pool of paint and dribble another colour on top.

Flicking paint: load a large brush with paint and flick it across the paper (make sure no-one is standing in the way). At first, the paint will flick across the paper in streaks but as the paint gets used up, it will start to leave specks.

Tip
If the paint bottles are heavy, give younger ones a bit of help. Support them in holding the bottle, but let them direct the movements so that they are creating their own lines and shapes.

Use for

A 'Jackson Pollock' abstract: Jackson Pollock was an American artist who created large abstract works using the 'drip and dribble' technique. His style is referred to as 'action painting' because it involves so much vigorous activity from the artist - quite apart from creating a picture full of movement. Try making your own Jackson Pollock action painting with a small group of children. Use a long strip of paper and move everybody around from time to time so that they can work on a different part of the paper. Add some other paint effects such as Spraying paint (*below*), Brush effects (*page 25*), Paint tracks (*page 31*) and Body part printing (*page 43*). Experiment with fluorescent, pearlescent or metallic paint on black paper for some striking results.

Night skies: create a starry sky by flicking a paint brush loaded with yellow paint across black paper. Do the first few flicks on scrap paper until you are getting specks rather than streaks of paint. Once the paint stars are dry, add planets made from smudged circles of chalk (*see Smudging and blending chalk and pastels/ Smudging, page 56*).

Spraying paint (3.5+)

Spraying paint across paper gives a subtle, misty effect and can be used to enhance a picture or create a stencilled pattern. You can buy specialised paint sprayers, but everyday equipment such as a nail brush and knife is just as effective.

You will need

• Ready mixed paint
• Water

Paint

- Saucers
- A nail brush or old toothbrush
- A blunt knife
- A plant sprayer
- Card or sturdy paper

What to do

Pour different coloured paint into the saucers. Dip the nail brush in the paint and pull the knife across the bristles so that the paint sprays onto the paper. If you want a more watery effect, thin the paint with a little water. Put watered down paint in the plant sprayer and spray across the paper. Experiment to create different effects:

Blending colours: spray one colour across another to create colour mixes, for example yellow across red to give an orange appearance or white across red to make pink.

Different backgrounds: experiment with different combinations of colour and background paper. Try pearlescent, fluorescent or metallic paint on black paper. Try spraying paint onto paper of the same colour, checking first that they are contrasting shades so that the paint shows up.

Different brushes: try different brushes – a nail brush, a toothbrush, a scrubbing brush, an old hair brush. Compare the results.

Plant sprayer: adjust the nozzle on the plant sprayer to produce a finer spray or a coarser spray. Compare the results.

Use for

Stencilling: cut out shapes from card, use tiny blobs of blu-tack to attach them to the paper and spray across the whole sheet of paper. When the paint is dry, peel off the pieces of card to reveal the shapes beneath. Use star, holly and Christmas trees stencils to make cards, gift tags and wrapping paper. Use small shapes to make decorative folders, book covers and mounts for other pictures.

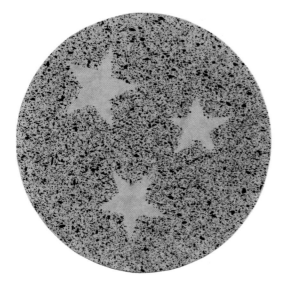

Stencilled stars

Weather pictures: try spraying white paint onto a grey background for a snowstorm or a misty day.

Landscapes and scenery: use shades of yellow, ochre and light brown to make a sandy beach. Try browny reds or greys to make the walls of buildings. Give mountains a 'distant' look by spraying with pale grey and violet.

Animals: spraying paint creates a natural effect that is useful for decorating animals. Try bright colours for tropical fish and butterflies, grey, white and a little black to make the thick, grainy skin of an elephant and greens and browns for toads or frogs.

Spraying with paint – protect your surroundings!

Spraying paint can be messy. Protect your surroundings by working inside a box. Cut one side from a large cardboard box and place the paper in the floor of the box before spraying. When using a brush and a knife, always pull the knife towards you to make sure the spray of paint goes across the paper rather than all over you!

Salty painting (3.5+)

Sprinkling salt on wet paint is a simple way to create some fabulous effects. You can try it with any age group.

You will need

- Ready mixed, powder paint or water colours
- Water
- Salt
- Thick brushes
- White cartridge paper

What to do

Mix up a watery paint solution. Using a thick brush, wash the thinned paint across the paper. Before the paint dries, sprinkle salt over the paper. Watch as the salt soaks up the wet paint, creating a mottled, crystalline effect. Once the paint is dry, you can either brush off all the salt or leave some of it attached to the paper. Experiment with different colours and thicknesses of paint, and try ordinary table salt and large grains of sea salt.

Use for

Sea pictures: salt painting works well for seascapes. Sprinkle it on shades of blue to create seawater and yellow, ochre and light browns to create sand. You can also use it to add texture to sea creatures.

Weather pictures: use salt on white paint to make snowstorms, snow capped mountains, icy ponds or misty scenes. Sprinkle salt onto shades of grey to make angry storm clouds.

Paint tracks (all ages)

Making tracks in paint is a simple form of printmaking that even the youngest children can explore.

Tractor Tracks by Belle (3)

You will need

- Ready mixed paint
- Saucers and teaspoons, one for each colour
- Tools for making tracks and patterns in the paint – pastry wheels, patterned rolling pins, toy tractors and other vehicles with patterned tyres
- Sturdy paper such as thin card or sugar paper

What to do

Using the teaspoons, drip the paint onto the paper. Experiment with mixing colours and make sure that there are plenty of thick blobs. Drive the toy tractors or roll pastry cutters through the paint to make tracks. Try making straight tracks, wavy tracks and curved tracks. As an alternative to driving through a blob of paint, try painting the wheels and making tracks across a clear piece of paper. Which technique do the children prefer?

Use for

Creating texture: use paint tracks to add texture to paintings of animals, buildings and landscapes.

Vehicle projects: make paint tracks across large sheets of paper and use to mount any work linked to vehicles or journeys.

Roller ball painting (all ages)

Rolling a ball through blobs of paint is a different way to create paint tracks. The ball is easier to control if you work inside a shallow box, although younger children may need some help with tilting the box from side to side.

Roller Ball Patterns by Sarah (5)

You will need

- Ready mixed paint
- Saucers and dessert spoons, one for each colour
- A shallow box or plastic tray with sides
- Sugar paper or cartridge paper, cut to fit the base of the box
- Spherical objects such as oranges or large marbles

What to do

Place a sheet of paper in the bottom of the box. Put a marble or orange in one of the saucers and roll it around with the spoon so that it gets covered with paint. Using the spoon, lift the marble out of the paint and drop it onto the paper. Roll the box from side to side so that the marble leaves painty tracks across the paper. Repeat the process with a different colour and observe how the colours blend.

Patchwork print patterns

Make a patchwork of paint patterns, to display on the wall and showcase the many different effects that you have tried. Cut out several squares of different coloured paper, all the same size. Prepare plenty of squares so that the children can produce as many paint effect samples as they wish. Include some or all of the following:

- Brush effects (*page 25*)
- Dribbling and flicking paint (*page 27*)
- Spraying paint (*page 28*)
- Salty painting (*page 30*)
- Paint tracks (*page 31*)
- Roller ball painting (*page 31*)
- Wet paper and watery paint effects (*page 34*)

The patchwork does not have to be completed in one session – you can build it up over a number of days or weeks. Encourage the children to experiment with the different techniques and combine them to make patterns. Try some of the following:

- A pattern of fans interspersed with paint dots.
- A background of sprayed paint with roller ball painting on top, in a contrasting colour.
- Paint tracks made through dribbled and flicked paint.
- Lines of brush effects (fans, lines, stippling) made with a paint loaded brush and placed next to a square of similar effects made with quite a dry brush.

If you give the children freedom to produce their own combinations of colour and pattern, you will be amazed at how creative they can be.

Use for

Decorative papers: roller ball painting can be used to decorate book covers, work folders, wrapping paper and paper for mounting work. While the paint is still wet, sprinkle on glitter to add a festive touch.

Cling film and laminate painting (all ages)

Cling film can be used in various ways to create some interesting paint effects. All age groups can try the following activities, but younger children need careful supervision to ensure that they don't put the cling film over their faces.

You will need

- Cling film, preferably the tougher variety designed for the freezer
- Laminate pouches
- Ready mixed paints in squeezy bottles
- Water colours
- Sturdy cartridge or watercolour paper

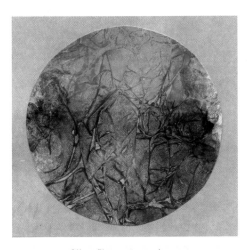

Cling film water colours

What to do

Ready mixed paints: drip thick blobs of paint directly from the bottle onto the paper. Place a sheet of cling film over the paint and use the fingers to merge and blend the blobs of paint together. Enjoy the cool, squidgy feel of the paint beneath the cling film! Gently lift the cling film off the paper and leave the painting to dry. To create a different effect, pull the paint into streaks by slowly dragging the cling film off the paper.

Water colours (7+): prepare some different coloured paint solutions. Although the paint needs to be quite watery, the colours should also be strong. Cover areas of the paper with different colours, allowing the paint to blend a little at the edges. Place a sheet of cling film over the paint while it is still wet. Move the cling film to form lots of creases and leave it in place while the paint dries. Once it is completely dry, gently peel off the film to reveal the attractive 'wrinkly' texture in the dry paint.

Laminate paintings: as an alternative to cling film, make a painting inside a laminate pouch. Open up the pouch and paint onto one side. Make sure the paint is not too thick, otherwise it will never dry. When the painting is finished, close the pouch and press the colours to spread and mix them.

Use for

Window Colours by Sarah (4)

Fiery scenes: cling film painting with red, yellow and orange ready mixed paints is great for creating flames, particularly if you drag the cling film off the paper to make flame-like streaks. When the paint is dry, stick on black squares and rectangles to represent buildings silhouetted against the fire. You can also turn the flames into a bonfire for a firework night picture.

Watery scenes: use blues, greens and a little brown and white ready mixed paint and drag the cling film sideways to create a river. Use as a background for pictures of fish, pond insects and other aquatic creatures.

Laminate painting window decal: tape a laminate pouch painting to a window pane. The light will shine through the colours, making them glow.

Wet paper and watery paint (4+)

Using thin, watery paint or painting on wet paper creates some interesting effects – and you can never be quite sure how the paint will behave when it comes into contact with the paper! Encourage the children to watch carefully as the paint forms its own patterns and shapes.

You will need

- Ready mixed paint
- Water colours
- Powder paint
- A water jar
- Teaspoons
- Containers for the paint
- Brushes, including a decorator's brush
- A sponge
- Watercolour paper
- Absorbent tissues, small pieces of sponges and cotton buds
- Drinking straws

What to do

There are various different ways to explore watery painting. Try the following:

Lines on wet paper: use a sponge or a decorator's brush to wet the surface of the paper. Brush lines of watercolour paint across the paper and watch as the paint runs

into the water. Experiment with stripes of different colours so that the colours bleed into each other.

Blobs on wet paper: use the same technique of painting on wet paper, but this time, paint blobs rather than stripes. Try dripping thick blobs of ready mixed paint directly from the bottle.

Lifting off wet paint: mix up some watery paint and paint a colour wash over a sheet of paper. While the paint is still wet, dab at the surface using damp tissues, a sponge or a cotton bud. This will lift off some of the paint to create a textured effect.

Dripping water: paint a strong colour wash over the surface of the paper. Using a teaspoon, drip some clean water on the paint and watch as it spreads to create patterns.

Painty puddles: drip pools of water onto the paper with a teaspoon or thick brush. Drop blobs of paint into the puddles and watch as the paint spreads to create swirling patterns.

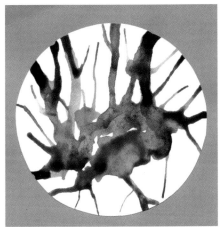

Blowing watery paint (6+): mix up some watery paint. Drip pools of paint onto the paper and blow hard through the straw until the paint disperses into spikes. Experiment with mixing two or three colours.

Sprinkling powder paint: wash the surface of the paper with water. Using your finger and thumb, sprinkle different colours of dry powder paint onto the surface of the paper. Some of the powder will absorb the water and turn into paint. Try blending the colours with a finger.

Blowing watery paint with a straw

> **Tip**
> *Work on watercolour paper to prevent the painting from wrinkling as it dries. If the paper does wrinkle, flatten it out by resting it under some heavy books for a day or two.*

Use for

Skies: painting stripes of blue on wet paper makes an effective sky. Paint several coats at the top of the paper to create a darker blue, gradually fading to a very pale blue at the horizon. Create clouds by dabbing at the wet paint with a damp tissue or a sponge.

Water: working on wet paper, paint stripes of blue and green with a little grey and brown to make a river or pond. Add to the watery effect by dripping clean water onto the paint.

Multi-coloured shapes: using a very faint pencil line, draw a shape on watercolour paper. Brush water all over the shape. Dab blobs of watery paint onto the wet shape so that the colours bleed into each other. This technique is good for Autumn leaves (use yellow,

orange, mustardy brown and a little green), rainbows (use stripes of red, orange, yellow, green, blue, indigo and violet), butterflies, birds and flowers.

Trees and twigs: use different shades of watery brown paint and blow the paint into spikes to make the branches and twigs of a tree.

Witches and monsters: use watery black or dark green paint and blow the paint into streaks to make the talons for a monster or a witch's straggly hair.

Fireworks: sprinkling dry powder paint onto wet paper creates the effect of a firework exploding into a mass of coloured stars.

Italian River by Joe (12)

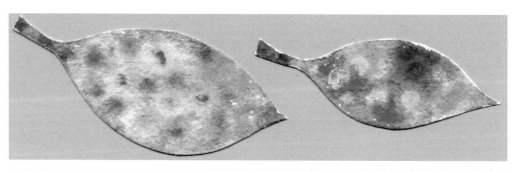

Autumn leaves

Pasty paint (5+)

Mixing up a paste from flour and paint is a quick and easy way of creating a thick textured medium that can be used to make patterns and prints.

You will need

- Ready mixed or powder paint
- Plain white flour
- An old tablespoon
- Thick brushes
- Containers for the paint
- Paint scrapers – combs, old toothbrushes, card strips cut with grooves and notches
- Sturdy cartridge paper or thin card
- Stiff card, such as the backs of cereal boxes

What to do

Mix together the flour and paint to make a paste. The paste can then be used in three main ways:

Pasty paint patterns: cut notches and grooves into stiff card strips. Brush the pasty paint across the surface of the paper and run the grooved card across the paint. The card will leave furrows in the thick paste. Experiment with wavy lines, zig-zags and criss-cross patterns. Try other tools such as old combs or toothbrushes.

Pasty paint textures: pasty paint can be used by younger children to create texture and relief patterns in the paint. Mix up a paste using approximately two parts paint to one part flour. Check that the paste is the right consistency to spread onto thin card. Dispense with the brush, and apply the paste to the card using fingers or flexible kitchen palette knives. Show the children how to mould the paste to create ridges and dents. Try blending different colours together.

Pasty paint prints: brush a thin layer of paste across the surface of the card. Using the thick end of a chopstick, draw a picture or pattern in the paste. Place a sheet of paper on the surface of the paste and press down gently. Carefully peel back the paper to reveal the pasty print. Experiment with different combinations of colour – try yellow paint on red paper, or white paint on black paper.

Tip
When making pasty prints, keep the layer of paste quite thin. If the paint is too thick, the paper will slip as you press it down and smudge the print. You also need to make sure the markings in the paste are wide enough to show up on the print.

Use for

Decorative papers: pasty paint patterns make effective book covers, folders and mounts for other work.

Van Gogh paintings: pasty paint can be used to create textured paintings in the style of Vincent Van Gogh. If you look closely at paintings such as The Sunflowers, you can see the texture in the thick oil paints. Young children can create a similar textured effect to Van Gogh by using pasty paint.

Printed snowman: use the pasty print technique to create a wintry scene. Mix up a paste from white paint and flour and work on black paper. Draw large snowflakes and a snowman shape. Once the paint has dried, stick on a scarf and carrot nose, cut from coloured paper.

Mixing up pasty paint

Different projects will need different thicknesses of paste. As a rough guide, mix one part flour to two or three parts paint. Add the flour a spoonful at a time until you have the right thickness. If in doubt, have a run through to check that your mixture is an appropriate consistency for the particular project.

PVA paint (4+)

Mixing paint with PVA glue gives the paint a thick, glossy quality. PVA paint can be used for lots of different projects, including comb patterns, PVA 'drizzles' and painting over the shiny, printed surface of a scrap box. For more information about PVA, see About glue *(page 61)*.

You will need

- PVA glue
- Ready mixed paint
- Powder paint
- Containers and teaspoons (for mixing)
- Coloured card (for backgrounds)
- Stiff card (for cutting into combs)
- Old combs
- Cling film

What to do

Mix the paint with the PVA glue. The ratio of paint to glue will depend on the nature of the project (*see Use for section, below*). Dry powder paint will give you the richest colour, although the mixing will take some time.

Use for

PVA paint comb patterns: for this activity, you will need a mixture of approximately one part ready mixed paint to one part glue. Brush the PVA paint over a sheet of stiff card and use cardboard combs to make patterns in the paint (*see Pasty paint / Pasty paint patterns, page 37*).

'Drizzle' decorations: mix the glue with powder paint and drizzle teaspoons of the coloured glue onto a sheet of cling film. Before the glue is completely dry, sprinkle on glitter. When the drizzles are set, peel off the cling film. Using a needle and thread, sew a loop through the decoration so that it can be hung up.

Rivers and ponds: use PVA glue to make rivers, ponds and lakes for a model landscape or farmyard. Draw a river shape on a stiff card or wood base. Paint the river with blue and green ready mixed or acrylic paint. Stick a watertight ridge of Plasticine around the boundaries of the shape and pour in a thick layer of PVA glue. Add a few small pebbles at the edges of the shape to give your river an authentic look. The glue will dry to form a clear watery surface over the paint.

Painting scrap boxes: PVA paint has good covering qualities. Use it to paint over the glossy, printed surfaces of scrap card and boxes.

Marbling (5+)

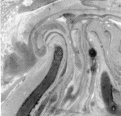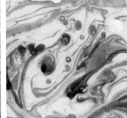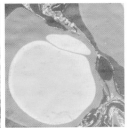

Marblling patterns

Marbling is easy to do and produces some very professional looking results. Although you can use any waterproof paints or inks, the best effect comes from specialised marbling inks, available from good art shops and schools suppliers.

You will need

- Marbling inks
- Thin paper such as copier paper
- A shallow container, such as a baking tray
- Chopsticks

What to do

Fill the container with water. Drip different coloured inks onto the surface of the water and gently drag them with a chopstick to create swirling patterns. Don't worry if the inks look a bit pale – their bright colours will show up once they have transferred to the paper. Carefully hold the sheet of paper flat on the surface of the water for about 15 seconds. Lift up the paper and turn it over. Keep the paper as level as possible to prevent the colours from running. Leave the marbling to dry on a flat surface. To make a different type of pattern, drip blobs of colour on top of each other and don't drag the inks with the chopstick.

> **Tip**
> *Younger children will need some help holding the paper on the surface of the water, turning it over swiftly and keeping it flat. If marbling is new to you, have a practice run through to get a 'feel' for the process.*

Use for

Decorative papers: marbling is perfect for decorating wrapping papers, book covers and mounts for other work.

Boxes, trays and pencil pots: use marbled paper for covering boxes, trays, pencil pots and other items (*see Cylinder pencil holder, page 68*).

Marbled sculpture: show off a collection of marbled patterns with a simple construction. Cover small cardboard cylinders or boxes with different papers and build them into a sculpture (*see Cylinder collage, page 66 and Collage with boxes, page 70*).

Marbled paper weaving: weave together strips of marbled paper (*see Card and paper weaving, page 79*). Combine different colours and designs.

Drying marbled paper

Oil based marbling inks take much longer to dry than water based paints. Make your marbled paper a few days before you plan to use it.

Bubble prints (4+)

Bubble printing is a less sophisticated version of marbling and is easier for little ones to manage.

You will need

- Paint, preferably powder paint, although ready mixed paint will also work
- Washing up liquid
- A shallow container such as a roasting tin
- A wooden spoon (for stirring)
- Straight drinking straws
- Cartridge paper

What to do

Mix the powder paint with water to the consistency of single cream. Add some washing up liquid so that you have a mixture of approximately one part washing up liquid to five parts paint. Pour the mixture into the shallow container. Using the straw, blow bubbles in the mixture. Hold the paper on top of the bubbles until they pop and leave their print on

the paper. Blow slowly to make just one or two large bubbles, or blow a little harder to create lots of little bubbles. Experiment with different coloured paints and papers.

> **Tip**
> *Watch younger children closely to ensure that they don't suck through the straw, rather than blow.*

Use for

Watery pictures: use a paint technique to create a watery effect background (*see Wet paper and watery paint, page 34*). Cut out the bubbles and stick them to the background. Add small individual bubbles to pictures of fish to make it look as though the fish is blowing bubbles.

Creatures: turn the bubbles into imaginary creatures, aliens and insects by adding felt pen or painted facial features, legs, tails and wings.

Hair dos: draw or paint faces. Cut out bubble prints and stick them onto the faces to make the hair.

Simple printing (all ages)

Printy Patterns by Sarah (4)

As long as an object is easy to hold, even the youngest children can have a go at printing. It may take a while for them to grasp the process. Be ready for little ones to 'paint' with the object as they learn the difference between printing and painting.

You will need

- Objects that make an interesting print and are easy to hold – cotton reels, half a carrot, ready cut sponge shapes, half potatoes (with cut handles – *see PRINTING WITH FRUIT AND VEG box, page 43*).
- Hand sized wooden blocks, sanded at the edges
- Small items with interesting shapes such as paper clips, hair grips, coins
- PVA glue
- Ready mixed paint
- Shallow saucers
- Flat sponges to fit inside the saucers
- Thick brushes
- Paper with a slightly absorbent surface, such as sugar paper

What to do

Preparing a printing pad: soak a flat sponge with water and wring it out so that it is just damp. Put the sponge in the saucer and squeeze on a blob of paint. Let the paint soak into the sponge to make a printing pad (if the paint is thick, give it a little help with a large paint brush). To use the printing pad, press an object onto the sponge so that the printing surface becomes covered with paint.

There are three main keys to successful printing:

Holding the object: get a firm and comfortable grip on the object. If an object is small or difficult to hold, it can be harder to control the printing process and the results may end up smudged. Glue fiddly objects, such as paper clips, to a hand sized block of wood (*see Card printing blocks, page 65*).

Applying the paint: make sure the surface of the item is covered with the right quantity of paint. Too much and the print will be splodgy, too little and the print will be faint. With some objects, the first print should be done on scrap paper to blot up the excess paint. Although a paint soaked printing pad is easy to use, small objects sometimes work better if the paint is applied with a brush.

Printing with the object: press the object firmly on the paper and hold it still. If the object is moved while it is on the paper, the print will smudge. As the object is lifted up off the paper, hold the paper down with one hand to stop it from sticking to the painty surface.

Once children have got the hang of printing, challenge them to find lots of different items to experiment with.

Use for

Wrapping paper and gift tags: choose some appropriate motifs, such as sponge stars and flowers, a heart cut into a half potato or cotton reels. Rule a faint grid of pencil lines on a large sheet of tissue paper and make a regular pattern of prints within the grid. Print a single motif on small squares of card to make matching gift tags. Give the paper and tags a Christmassy feel by adding PVA glue to the paint and sprinkling glitter onto the prints.

Writing paper and envelopes: printing can be used to decorate writing paper and envelopes. Print lines of motifs along the top and bottom or down the side of a sheet of paper. Decorate matching envelopes, making sure there is enough space left to write the address. Tie the paper and envelopes into a bundle with ribbon and present to parents or grandparents as a gift.

Decorating borders: printing is particularly effective for decorating borders on picture mounts or the pages of a home made book.

Pictures: use prints to create pictures. Encourage children to use their own ingenuity in creating a tree, an animal or a house made up of different prints. For example, a large apple tree could be printed with real leaves and apple halves.

Printing with fruit and veg

Cut a half potato into a relief shape for printing. With a sharp knife, cut down into the surface of the potato and then slice across, to leave the printing area raised. Make half potatoes easy for children to hold. Cut a wedge from either side of the potato dome to make a handle.

Various fruit and vegetables are good for printing. Try a half mushroom, onion, broccoli floret or lemon. Leave juicy items such as lemons to dry out slightly before printing.

Body part printing (all ages)

Animal Paradise by Ellie (8)

Printing with different parts of the body is great fun and easy to do. Hands, feet and finger tips are the obvious ones, but if you and your children are feeling adventurous, how about arm prints, fist prints or even nose prints? All you need is a bit of imagination – and some soap and water nearby!

You will need

- Ready mixed paint
- Shallow containers or saucers for the paint
- Thick brushes
- Sugar paper
- A bowl of warm water, soap and towel

What to do

Hand prints: using a brush, cover the palm and fingers with paint and press down firmly on the paper. Experiment with different hand shapes: try spreading out the fingers, or holding them close together. Older children with sufficient control of the fingers can try stretching out just the thumb and little finger, or separating the thumb and index fingers from the other three fingers.

Foot prints: spread a large sheet of paper across the floor. Paint the soles of the children's feet and hold the paper down while they make their foot prints. Try tiptoeing across the paper and comparing the results with a full foot print. Children who don't like having their feet painted can make wellie prints, instead.

Finger prints: dip a fingertip into a saucer of ready mixed paint and press it on the paper to make oval shaped prints. To see the lines on the finger prints, press the finger onto an ink pad (although the ink is not always easy to wash off).

> **Tip**
> *Try painting stripes and splodges of different colour on the hands and feet, and making rainbow effect prints. As the paint gets used up, look at how the appearance of the hand or foot print changes.*

Use for

Animals: turn hand prints into animal pictures. Spread out the fingers and thumb to represent four legs and a tail and add markings with finger prints. Place two hand prints side by side to make a bird in flight. Use a thin, black pen to turn finger prints into insects. Create a group picture of a fish, with overlapping hand prints to represent the scales. Use fishy colours such as pale blue, pale green and grey, and add a little silver glitter to make the fish scales gleam.

Trees: hand prints make good leaves for a large tree. Use reds, yellows, oranges and browns to represent autumn leaves. Use wax crayon bark rubbings to make the trunk (*see Wax rubbings, page 50*).

Funny foot prints: cut out foot prints and stick them up the wall and across the ceiling. Who's been walking across the ceiling ...?

Funny hand prints: cut out brown, grey or black hand prints and stick one or two on mirrors, windows and other surfaces. Who's been leaving dirty hand prints everywhere ...?

Baby cards: a painty foot print makes a delightful personalised card that even the tiniest baby can participate in. Choose pretty colours, print onto the front of a folded card and stick stars around the print.

Polystyrene tile prints (6+)

The soft surface of a polystyrene tile can easily be engraved to make a printing block. The process is similar to that of lino cut printing, but without having to use a sharp cutting tool. Unlike printing with simple objects, this enables children to draw and print their own designs.

You will need

- Pencils and pieces of white paper, cut to the same size as the tiles (for planning a design)
- Polystyrene tiles
- Felt pens
- Sharp pencils
- Pieces of card, cut slightly larger than the tiles (for the print)

Paint

- Large masonry nails
- Ready mixed paint
- Brushes
- Rolling pins (optional)

What to do

Plan a design using a pencil and a sheet of paper cut to the same size as the polystyrene tile. Emphasise that the design must be bold and simple with not too much intricate detail. Copy the design onto the tile using a felt pen and gouge out the lines with a masonry nail. Check that the grooves are wide and deep, otherwise they will not show up on the print. Cover the whole surface of the tile with paint and press it down on the printing card. If the tile is quite large, roll over it with a rolling pin to ensure that every part is printed. Carefully peel off the tile to reveal the print.

Use for

Book marks: cut the polystyrene tile into a long, thin rectangle and gouge out a design. Print onto a strip of card, leaving a margin around the edge of the print. Using a hole puncher, make a hole in the bottom of the card and tie on a strip of ribbon to make a tag.

Book covers: unlike printing with objects, polystyrene tiles enable children to create their own designs. Ask the children to come up with a design to reflect the content of a homemade book and use a polystyrene tile print to create a professional looking cover. Cut the tile to fit the shape and size of the cover.

Chapter 3

Wax crayons, chalk and pastels

About wax crayons

Wax crayons are cheap and versatile. Their vibrant colours and chunky shapes make them perfect for babies and older children can use them to create a wide range of different art and craft effects. Unlike a pencil, the entire length of a wax crayon can be used for colouring in, and you can make different marks by cutting notches into the wax. Wax crayons are also water resistant and can be melted at quite low temperatures which makes them great for making wax resist paintings (*see page 52*) and melted wax patterns (*see page 56*).

Wax crayons come in various shapes and sizes, ranging from short chubby sticks to long, thin plastic crayons that can be sharpened with a pencil sharpener. You can get a wide assortment of different colours and types, including metallic, glitter, rainbow stripes and skin tone packs. Make sure that you invest in good quality crayons. The wax should leave a strong, bright mark on the paper. Cheaper crayons can result in rather thin, pale marks and they are not so easy or satisfying to use.

About chalk and pastels

Chalk also comes in many different shapes and sizes. For little ones, you can get short, stubby sticks and for children with gripping difficulties you can buy egg-shaped chalk. For drawing on outdoor surfaces, try the large, washable playground sticks. Most children love the satisfying experience of chalking on a blackboard. If possible, have a free standing blackboard, constantly available in your home or setting, so that children can explore drawing with chalk whenever they wish. For more permanent art work, chalk can be used on sturdy papers such as sugar paper or thin card. Choose dark shades to set off the glowing colours of the chalk. Chalk is also uniquely smudgy which can create some wonderfully effective results.

For older children, pastels are the next step. Pastels come in two types – chalk pastels and oil pastels. Chalk pastels are a finer version of blackboard chalk whereas oil pastels have an 'oily' texture, as their name suggests. Chalk pastels have a dry, smudgy quality. Oil pastels do not smudge in the same way and the oil content in the pastel lends a richness and a glow to their colours.

About paper for wax and chalk

You can use any paper for wax crayons, whereas chalk and pastels tend to work best on a robust paper with a slightly rough surface. Use sugar paper or buy special pastel paper, which is like a thick sugar paper and comes in various muted colours. Chalks and pastels also work well on textured papers. Look out for pastel paper with a stippled surface, sometimes called Ingres paper. As with all art media, experiment with different coloured backgrounds. Wax doesn't always show up particularly well on darker papers, whereas most chalks look effective against black or dark blue.

Wax crayons are fun because ...

Even babies can draw with them.
They have bright, jewel like colours.
You can use them to make wax rubbings.
You can use them to make paper batiks.
You can make melt them between sheets of paper to make stained glass windows.

Chalk is fun because ...

You can use it on a blackboard.
You can quickly rub it out if you don't like your drawing.
You can smudge the colours.
You can make attractive colour blends.

Activities

Wax crayon effects (4+)

Wax crayons can be used in many different ways to create some unique effects. Try the following techniques - and see how many more ideas you and your children can come up with.

You will need

• Wax crayons
• Metal tools such as screwdrivers (for making marks in wax)
• A sharp knife
• White cartridge paper or sugar paper

What to do

Wax engravings: rub a thick layer of wax on the paper and cover with a second layer, using a contrasting colour. Scratch patterns into the wax with a screwdriver. Experiment with

different colour combinations to see which gives the best effect.

Shading with wax: hold a crayon on its side and create a misty effect by rubbing the paper with the entire length of the crayon. Try shading one colour on top of another, always using the darker colour first.

Different pressures: experiment with the different effects you can get when you press hard or gently with the crayon.

Blending colours: make new colours by rubbing one colour on top of another. Always start off with the darker colour, such as green, and finish with the lighter colour such as yellow.

Wax circles: use crayons with a round, flat end. Hold the flat end against the paper and twist the crayon to create circles.

Grooved crayons: using a sharp knife, make notches in the side of a crayon. Rub the entire length of the crayon along the paper to leave a pattern of lines. Experiment with thick and thin notches, set close together and far apart.

Use for

Tortoise by William (11)

Tortoises and pineapples: small wax engravings can be used to decorate objects with tessellating polygon patterns, such as tortoiseshells or pineapples. Draw several polygons on a piece of paper and cover with two different coloured layers of wax. Using a screwdriver, engrave stars, spirals and other patterns into the wax. Cut out the polygons and stick them onto a card tortoiseshell or pineapple.

Wax crayon patchworks: make a patchwork of different wax crayon effects (*see Pencil effects / Patchwork pencil patterns, page 12*). Use the patchwork as a wall display and a reminder of the different techniques that children can use in their wax drawings.

Wax scratch cards (4+)

Make scratch cards from wax crayons and black paint. Older children can try making their own cards.

You will need

- Good quality wax crayons in a range of colours
- A5 sized pieces of stiff white card
- Black ready mixed paint
- A large paint brush
- Metal tools such as screwdrivers, large masonry nails or blunt ended darning needles

What to do

Making the scratch cards: colour in the surface of the card with wax crayons. Use lots of different colours and press hard so that the layer of wax is thick. Make sure that no white card shows through. Paint over the wax with the black paint and leave to dry.

Using the scratch cards: scratch patterns into the black paint with a metal tool such as a screwdriver. The screwdriver will scrape away the paint to reveal the multi-coloured wax surface beneath.

Use for

Night lights: use wax scratch cards to make pictures of lights or fireworks – Bonfire Night, Diwali, Christmas lights.

Patchwork patterns: make a large, square wax scratch card and draw a rough grid in the dry paint. Fill in the squares with different patterns such as cross hatching and dots (see Pencil effects, page 11)

Ancient art: wax scratch cards work well for designs inspired by traditional art. Look at some Greek pottery or artifacts from North American and aboriginal cultures. Use cards made with earthy colours such as browns, oranges, terracottas and sandy yellow ochre.

Frames and borders: cut out a card frame or mark out a border on a large sheet of mounting paper. Turn the frame or border into a scratch card and decorate with triangles, rectangles and other linear patterns.

Oil pastel scratch cards

You can make scratch cards with oil pastels, as well as wax crayons. This will give you a greater range of colours for projects such as Ancient art.

Wax rubbings (3+)

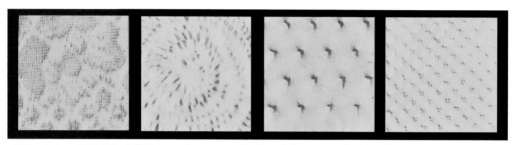

Wax rubbing samples – lace, rattan mat, cheese grater, nutmeg grater

The craft technique of making a wax rubbing is simple but effective. Young children love to watch the pattern emerge, as if by magic!

You will need

- Chunky wax crayons
- Thin paper such as copier paper, in a range of colours
- Various objects with textured surfaces

What to do

Place a sheet of paper over a textured surface or object and rub across the paper with a wax crayon. Watch carefully as the textured wax pattern appears on the paper. Younger ones may need some help holding the paper still while they make their rubbing. If you are working with flat objects such as a textured floor tile, tape the paper to the surface to keep it steady.

Use for

A cityscape collage: cut different rubbings into rectangles and squares and stick them onto a card background to make a skyscraper scene. Choose rubbings to suggest the various textures of the buildings, and encourage the children to think about appropriate colours for a city scene – granite greys, brick reds and sandy yellows.

Animal collage: the textures and patterns created by wax rubbing work well for animal collages. Use brown and black wax on yellow paper and dark brown wax on pale brown or grey. The rough texture of bark makes good fur; use a cheese grater or a colander for spots and markings; use wicker baskets or rattan mats for stripes.

Landscape collage: make a traditional English patchwork of fields with squares and rectangles in different shades of green and brown. Use corrugated card and brown wax to make ploughed fields and roughly textured wallpaper rubbings to represent grassy fields. Add trees and bushes made from bark and leaf rubbings.

Decorative papers: wax rubbings can be used to decorate the covers and pages of a handmade book, or as mounts for other work.

Cityscape at Night by Ellie (8)

Objects for wax rubbing

The following objects make good wax rubbings:

- Corrugated card • Leaves with raised veins • Bricks • Pieces of bark • Coins
- Wicker baskets • Rattan and wicker mats • Textured tiles • Cheese graters
- Metal or plastic sieves • Colanders • Lace • Paper doilies • Textured wallpaper

Brass rubbing

Brass rubbing is an ancient craft. In medieval and Tudor times, noblemen were commemorated with engraved brass plates depicting themselves and their families. Although few churches allow you take rubbings directly from the plates, you can find resin copies in brass rubbing centres. Visiting a brass rubbing centre makes a great day out with a small group of children from age four upwards. Most centres provide paper and wax for a small charge.

Wax bundles (5+)

Once children get the hang of drawing with a wax crayon bundle, they love creating multi-coloured 'shadow' drawings.

You will need

- Wax crayons
- Elastic bands
- Large sheets of cartridge paper
- Tape

What to do

Tie at least three crayons into a tight bundle with an elastic band. Tap the crayons on the surface of the table to make sure that the points are level. Choose contrasting colours such as yellow, red and blue, or colours that go together such as pink, purple and turquoise. Tape a large sheet of paper to the floor or the table top and let the children enjoy the effect of creating several 'shadow' marks with just the one implement.

Use for

Wax resist: encourage the children to press hard and then paint over the markings with thin paint to make a wax resist pattern (*see below*).

Weather and the seasons: the 'movement' in wax bundle scribbles can be used to reflect different seasonal weather. Make white, dark grey and pale blue scribbles on light grey paper as a background for work on wind or snowstorms. Make orange, red and brown scribbles on yellow paper as a background for work on Autumn leaves.

Wax resist paintings (3+)

Wax is an unusual art medium in that it is water resistant and can be used in various ways to produce some interesting effects.

You will need

- Wax crayons
- White candles
- White cartridge paper
- Ready mixed or powder paint
- Water
- A thick brush
- A damp cloth

Under the Sea by Toby (7), Jacob (6), Daniel (6) and Sofie (6)

What to do

Thin the paint with water. Make wax crayon drawings or patterns on a sheet of white cartridge paper. Encourage the children to press as hard as they can and go over lines to make sure they are not too thin. When the drawing has been completed, wash over it with the watered down paint. The wax will resist the paint and the drawing will show through. Substitute a white candle for the wax if you want the drawing to appear colourless. If the children have coloured in large areas, they may need to wipe the paint off the wax with a damp cloth.

Tip
Wax resist pictures can also be made with oil pastels. Like wax crayons, they are water resistant.

Use for

Night time scenes: wax resist with dark blue paint works well for pictures of night time scenes. For a starry sky, use yellow wax. Use a range of colours for a fairground scene, fireworks, seaside illuminations or Christmas lights.

Ghostly pictures: use a white candle with a blue wash to make pictures of ghosts and ghouls. The candle wax may not transfer as well as the wax crayon, so make sure the

Ghosts! by Joe (9)

children press hard. Encourage them to keep their pictures straightforward – it can be difficult to see the candle wax on the paper, and they are less likely to lose their way with a large, simple image. The paint needs to be very watery, otherwise it will cover the candle wax.

Backgrounds: washing over a wax drawing with paint is an easy way to fill in a background. Make brightly coloured wax drawings of fish and wash over with blue and green to make the sea; make drawings of birds, clouds and a rainbow, and wash over with sky blue; make drawings of jungle or farmyard animals and wash over with shades of green.

Decorative papers: the wax resist technique can be used to make decorative paper for home made book covers, pages or mounts for other work. Create a design using simple motifs, or use the wax bundle technique (*page 52*) to make swirling rainbow patterns.

Paper batik (4+)

Batik is a traditional craft that involves making a design with melted wax on fabric. The fabric is then dyed, with the wax acting as a resist. The classic crackled effect is created by crunching up the fabric to make cracks in the dry wax. Try this batik inspired activity with paper and wax crayons.

You will need

- Wax crayons
- Thin paper, such as a lightweight cartridge or copier paper
- Ready mixed paint in dark colours such as blue, dark red or green
- A thick brush
- Paper towels

What to do

Make a wax crayon drawing. Encourage the children to cover the whole surface of the paper with wax and to press hard so that the layers of wax are thick.

When the drawing is finished, crumple up the picture, taking care not to rip the paper. Smooth out the paper and crumple it up two or three more times to make cracks in the wax.

Smooth the paper out and paint over the picture with the ready mixed paint. Make sure the paint is brushed into the cracks in the wax.

Rinse the paper under the tap, working quickly but carefully - the aim is to wash off the surface paint without soaking the paper too much.

Spread the picture on paper towels and leave to dry. The paper should dry quite flat. If it is very crumpled you can place it between two sheets of newspaper and smooth it with a warm iron.

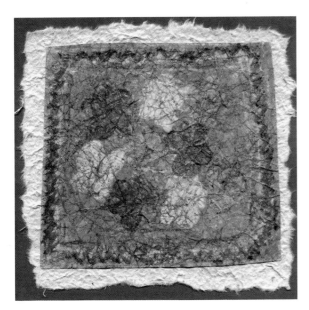

Batik Flowers by Rachel (11)

Use for

Flowers and plants: the traditional, crackled appearance of batik works well for decorative pictures of flowers, plants and leaves. Robust, handmade paper makes an effective mount for paper batiks.

Melted wax pictures (3+)

Apart from being water resistant, wax can also be melted. This activity uses up all those tiny wax stubs that have become too small for the children to draw with.

You will need

- Ends of wax crayons
- A large pencil sharpener
- A sharp knife and cutting board (for adult use only)
- Sturdy paper such as sugar paper or cartridge paper
- An iron and ironing board
- An old tea towel

What to do

Using the sharp knife and pencil sharpener, turn the wax crayon ends into small chunks and shavings. Sprinkle the wax pieces onto a sheet of paper. Make sure that you have different colours clumped together so that they will blend when melted.

Lay a second sheet of paper on top, cover the paper with the tea towel and iron across the tea towel. The hot iron will melt the wax to create interesting patterns and colour mixes. Before the wax hardens, peel the sheets of paper apart to reveal two similar patterns.

Tip

Some wax crayons are specially designed to be 'non-melt'. Check the packaging to make sure that you are using traditional crayons for this project.

Use for

Melted wax window decal: cut out two identical rectangles or diamonds from greaseproof paper. Sprinkle wax chunks and shavings onto one of the shapes and lay the second shape on top of the wax. Cover with a tea towel and smooth with a warm iron until the wax has melted. Leave the wax to harden, 'gluing' the two greaseproof shapes together (add a few dabs of PVA glue if necessary). Edge the shapes with strips of black card and hang in the window to make a stained glass decal.

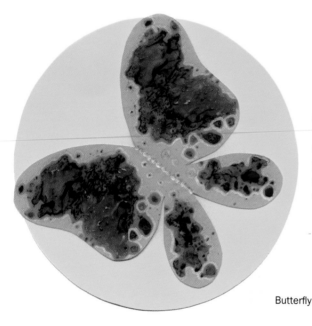

Fish, birds and butterflies: melted wax patterns are effective for anything that needs a richly coloured decoration. Cut the paper into butterfly, bird or fish shapes before sprinkling on the wax and ironing.

Butterfly

Smudging and blending chalk and pastels (4+)

It is well worth putting up with a bit of mess in return for the wonderful, smudgy colour blends that can be created with chalk.

You will need

- Different coloured chalks, or chalk pastels for older children
- Sturdy paper such as cartridge paper or pastel paper
- Cotton wool balls
- Cotton buds

What to do

Try the following effects:

Shading with chalk holding the
stick of chalk on its side

Shading with chalk: hold a stick of chalk on its side and rub it across the paper to create a grainy effect. The shading can be left as it is, or you can create a smoother appearance by smudging with fingers or cotton wool. Make an interesting pattern by using a range of colours and rubbing the chalks in different directions.

Blending colours: rub a light colour (such as yellow) onto the paper. Cover with a second darker colour (such as blue) and blend the two colours with the fingers, a cotton wool ball or cotton bud. You can also try this colour blending effect using the side of the chalk.

Chalk comets

Smudging: draw lines, cross hatching (*see page 11*), circles, spirals and other shapes. Smudge the markings with a finger or cotton bud. Make a small dot, pressing as hard as possible so that the chalk is thick. Using a quick movement with the finger, smudge in just the one direction to give the dot a comet-like tail.

Use for

Fireworks: smudged chalk on black or dark blue paper is great for firework pictures. Stab the chalk against the paper to make the stars of a rocket; draw large stars to make sparklers; draw spirals to make Catherine wheels. Carefully smudge all the markings with a finger or cotton wool bud.

Planets: blended chalk is good for creating the misty, slightly mysterious look of planets in the night sky. To make the planets, cut out circles of sturdy paper. Choose two or three colours such as blue and green, or yellow, orange and red. Draw spirals of chalk on the circles and then smudge round and round with a finger to create a smooth, circular effect. Make a starry sky background by flicking yellow paint onto black paper (*see page 56*). Once the paint is dry, stick on the chalk planets.

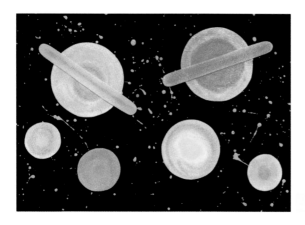

The Planets by Rachel (11)

Weather effects: chalk is very effective for creating weather pictures such as mist or snowstorms. To make a misty background, rub the side of a white chalk stick across pale grey paper. To make a snowstorm, stab white chalk against the paper and smudge slightly with a finger.

Autumn trees: chalk is a great for drawing Autumn trees because you can easily blend different shades of red, orange and yellow. Rub areas of colour onto the paper to represent the tree's foliage. Blend the colours at the edges by smudging with a finger and add hatching in dark green or brown to create detail.

Spraying chalk and pastel drawings

Chalk or chalk pastel drawings are easily smudged. You can buy special fixative spray from art shops to spray over the drawings. This 'sets' them and prevents them from smudging. A 'home made' alternative is to spray the pictures with hair spray.

Powdered chalk (4+)

It is the dry, dusty quality of chalk that makes it so 'smudgable'. Crush old bits of chalk to make colourful dust and explore some different ways of using this interesting substance.

You will need

- Ends of chalk
- Scrap paper (for crushing the chalk)
- White cartridge paper
- String
- A wooden board
- A hammer and nail
- A heavy tablespoon

What to do

Sprinkling and
smudging chalk dust

Sprinkling chalk dust: place the bits of chalk between two sheets of scrap paper and crush with the back of a heavy tablespoon. Sprinkle the dust randomly onto a sheet of white paper and rub with the fingers to create powdery patterns. When the picture is finished, shake off any loose bits of chalk.

Chalk dust
on wet paper

Chalk dust on wet paper: try sprinkling the chalk chunks and dust on wet paper. Experiment with mixing different colours and use a finger to make patterns in the soggy chalk dust.

Twanging string: hammer a nail into a wooden board and tie the end of the string around the nail's head. Run sticks of chalk along the string until it is thick with chalk dust. Place a sheet of white paper beneath the string. Hold the string taut and twang it so that the dust flicks onto the paper.

Drawing with wet chalk

You can change the quality of chalk by using it in conjunction with water and other liquids. Try soaking the chalk in milk or a sugar solution (about 50g sugar to 200ml water). The liquid will make the colours glow. You can also experiment with drawing on wet paper.

Chapter 4

Card, textured paper and papercraft

About card

Card comes in many different colours and weights. As well as buying it from stationers, school suppliers and art shops, you can also salvage food packaging and other scrap materials. It ranges from lightweight coloured card to stiff, triple-layered card cut from cardboard boxes. It is a versatile medium that can be used for collage, constructing models and mounting other work.

Coloured card is an essential part of any art cupboard. Thanks to its stiffer texture, it is easier to cut than paper. It is also less likely to wrinkle when you glue it onto a background, and its strong, even colour makes for eye-catching collages. Mounting artwork is another use for coloured card. Try double or even triple mounting, combining colours that complement each other and set off the picture.

Card comes in different weights, measured according to grams per square metre (gsm). Lightweight card has a weight of between 160 and 200gsm. For a medium card, go for a weight of between 200 and 350gsm. Check that you are buying card with an appropriate strength and stiffness for a particular project. There are also lots of different colours and finishes available, including fluorescent, metallic, pearlescent and patterned card, holographic card (expensive but stunning), bright colours, pastel colours and the endlessly useful black.

Scrap card materials are great, old cereal boxes are an inexpensive source. If you want to paint the glossy, printed surface of a cereal box, use ready mixed or powder paint thickened with PVA glue. Card cut from cereal and other food containers tends to be quite thin. For a more heavy duty card, use large cardboard packing boxes. This type of card often has a corrugated inner layer, which adds texture to a collage. Its strength and thickness also make it suitable as a base for models, or as a background for heavy work such as fabric collage (*see page 122*).

Smaller card boxes and tubes can be left intact and used for relief collage and scrap models. Herbs, tea and stock cubes all come in small, sturdy boxes, and the inner tubes from paper towels offer an endless source of cardboard cylinders.

About textured paper

As with 'card', the category of 'textured paper' covers a huge range of possibilities. Start a collection of textured papers, you will be amazed at how many different textures and patterns you can find.

Handmade paper should be at the core of any collection. Many art and craft shops sell a good selection of different papers, including packs of small off-cuts for collage. Handmade paper ranges from heavy papers with a strong wrinkly texture, to delicate handmade tissues. Some papers also have decorative bits and pieces added during the production process. Look out for papers made with flower petals, skeleton leaves, fabric and vegetable fibres.

Wallpaper is another good source of textured paper. Make a collection of papers with a regular pattern, flocked papers and woodchip paper (anaglypta). A plain coloured paper with an irregularly raised surface makes a good alternative paper for painting. You don't have to buy the whole roll – a sample may be all you need. Always check that ready-pasted paper is not potentially toxic, and supervise younger children working with woodchip paper.

Corrugated paper has a unique texture, with its regular lines of ridges and grooves. It is particularly good for printing and making textured wax rubbings, as well as collage and model making.

Other textured papers include good quality writing paper and specialised painting and pastel paper. Look out for linen writing paper with a delicate woven texture, or pastel and watercolour paper with a stippled surface (sometimes referred to as Ingres paper). Both these types of paper are quite expensive, so save them for special projects.

About glue

White PVA craft glue is the most versatile and effective for collage and model making. Although it is a thick, opaque white liquid in the bottle, it dries to a clear finish. This means that the children can use lots of glue in their artwork, without it spoiling the end result. It is also strong enough to hold heavier collage and model making items, including fabric, stone and wood.

PVA can also be watered down and brushed over clay models, paintings and other items to create a gentle, low gloss glaze and, unlike craft varnish, even young children can use it to do their own varnishing. It can also be blended with ready mixed or powder paint to create a thick, glossy paint with excellent covering qualities. It can be spread to a thin layer with a finger, a brush or a glue spatula, or it can be dribbled to create thick trails and blobs. If you work on clingfilm, you can peel off the dried glue shapes to create some interesting hanging decorations (*see PVA paint, page 38*).

Other glues include wallpaper paste, solid glue sticks and glue pens. Wallpaper paste is cheap but check that it doesn't contain toxic fungicides. Although it is fine for lightweight paper collage, it is not strong enough for heavier items such as stiff card or fabric. Solid glue sticks are convenient and clean to use but they often don't last very long and they lose some of their sticking power when they start to dry out. Glue pens are also convenient but check that the glue is flowing freely before giving them to the children. Younger ones may need some help with squeezing out the glue.

Why card?

Card is great for art and craft because:

- It comes in lots of different colours
- It comes in lots of different thicknesses and weights
- You can use it for collage
- You can use it for models
- You can use it for backgrounds
- Don't throw away scrap card – turn it into something beautiful!

Why textured paper?

Textured paper is great for art and craft because:

- You can use it for collage
- You can use it to make wax rubbings
- You can use it for printing
- You can use it to decorate models
- You can paint on it
- Even the simplest collage is more interesting when you use textured paper.

Activities

Geometric card shapes (all ages)

Geometric shapes such as squares, circles and triangles can be used in various different ways to make interesting collage pictures.

You will need

- Different types of card such as lightweight coloured card, corrugated card and card cut from cardboard boxes
- Scissors
- PVA glue
- Sturdy card (for the background)

What to do

Try the following ideas:

Shape collage: cut out lots of geometric shapes from coloured card and turn them into a collage. Children can either make an abstract pattern or use the shapes to create pictures.

Higgledy Piggledy by Michael (10) and Rachel (11)

Relief shape collage: cut out geometric shapes from heavyweight pieces of card such as corrugated card and cardboard boxes. Arrange the shapes on a stiff card background and stick them on with PVA glue. Encourage the children to experiment with the composition of their collage. Suggest that they glue shapes on top of each other to make higgledy piggledy piles. Try painting or decorating the card shapes and experiment with different coloured backgrounds.

3-D towers: cut out lots of squares, rectangles or triangles. Make each shape a little larger than the one before to create a series. Glue the shapes on top of each other, starting with the largest and ending with the smallest. The finished result should look like the bird's eye view of a tower. Experiment with different thicknesses of card and try combining colours and shapes.

Use for

Exploring geometric shapes: cut out lots of geometric shapes and challenge the children to make new shapes – two squares to make a rectangle, four little squares to make a big square, three triangles to make a trapezium, two trapeziums to make a hexagon, six triangles to make a hexagon.

Shape patterns: cut out lots of small rectangles, squares, circles, triangles and other shapes from different coloured card. Arrange the shapes in rows across a rectangle of card. Mix colours and shapes to add to the decorative effect – a line of small green squares interspersed with turquoise kites, for example.

Shape pictures: use cut-out card shapes as the inspiration for various pictures – turn diamonds into kites, squares and rectangles into houses, trapeziums into boats and roofs, circles and polygons into people. Challenge the children to come up with as many different ways of using a particular shape as possible. Add details with cut-out card or felt pens.

Tips for gluing

Very young children find it easier to put a blob of glue on the paper and then place their collage shape or item on top of the glue. Older children can spread glue directly onto a cut-out shape, before positioning it on the paper.

If you are working with PVA, use a finger or glue spatula to spread the glue as thinly as possible.

Once a cut-out shape has been glued to the background, place a sheet of thin paper over the shape and smooth across it to press out any wrinkles.

Sometimes, a paper shape will be a bit wrinkly once it has been glued onto a background. Put the collage in a heavy book so that it will dry flat. Make sure there are no traces of glue on the edge of the shape, otherwise the collage will stick to the book.

Show older children how to stick down the edges of a shape, without the glue oozing out from underneath. Glue the shape to a collage background, leaving the edges unstuck. Spread glue over the end of a thin card strip. Slide the strip under the edges of the shape to transfer the glue from the strip to the underneath of the shape. Pull out the strip and smooth over the shape with a sheet of thin paper.

Don't be afraid to use lots of PVA glue to stick awkward or heavy objects – the glue will dry to a clear finish!

Card rubbings (3.5+)

Make a collage from cut-out card shapes and use it as a panel for taking wax rubbings. The outline of the different shapes will show up on the rubbing.

You will need

- Two sheets of card
- Scissors
- PVA glue
- Thin paper such as copier paper
- Masking tape
- Wax crayons

What to do

Cut out some shapes from one of the sheets of card and stick them onto the second sheet of card. Younger children can cut out random shapes. Older children can cut out geometric shapes or shapes to build into a picture – for example, a house, an animal, a vehicle or a landscape. Tape a sheet of thin paper over the collage and use a wax crayon to take a rubbing.

Use for

Book covers: when you make a book with the children based on a theme, create a cover for it by making a suitable card collage and taking a wax rubbing. Double or triple mount the picture on sheets of coloured card, interspersed with a wax rubbing pattern (*see Wax rubbings, page 50*). Use the mounted picture to decorate the cover of the book.

Greetings cards: double or triple mount a small card rubbing picture on several mounts and turn it into a greetings card.

Card printing blocks (4+)

Christmas card made with a card printing block

Cut a single sheet of card into different shapes and glue the shapes to a chunk of wood to make a printing block.

You will need

- Card
- Scissors
- PVA glue
- Wood blocks
- Sugar paper for the printing

What to do

Saw a beam of wood into blocks and sand the edges to get rid of any splinters. Cut the card into shapes, spread PVA glue across the surface of the wood block and stick on the shapes. Brush paint onto the shapes and use the block to make prints (*for more on printing, see page 40*).

> **Tip**
> *To make a quick card printing block for older children, attach a blob of blu-tack to the back of the card shape and use as a handle.*

Use for

Wrapping paper and gift tags: rule a faint grid of pencil lines on a large sheet of tissue paper and make a regular pattern of card block prints within the grid. Print a single motif on small squares of card to make matching gift tags. Add a Christmassy touch by mixing PVA glue with the paint and sprinkling glitter onto the prints.

Writing paper and envelopes: use card block motifs to decorate writing paper and envelopes. Print lines of small motifs along the top and bottom or down the side of the writing paper. Decorate matching envelopes, leaving enough space for the address. Tie ribbon around the paper and envelopes to make an attractive handmade gift.

Decorating borders: card block printing is particularly effective for decorating borders on picture mounts or the pages of a home made book.

Book marks: make a pattern of card shapes on a rectangular shaped wood block. Print onto a strip of card, leaving a margin around the edge of the print. Using a hole puncher, make a hole in the bottom of the card and tie on a length of ribbon or a silk tassel.

Tip
Printing with scrap card - if you are using cereal box card to make your card printing block, remember that it is easier to print with the plain, matt side of the card. Make sure you stick the glossy, printed surface of the card to the wood block.

Cylinder collage (3+)

Card cylinders can be used to create some interesting collage pictures. You can either use ready made cylinders such as sweet tubes and paper towel holders, or you can roll your own tubes from rectangles of thin card.

You will need

- A variety of card tubes
- Thin card or sugar paper (for rolling tubes)
- Patterned paper (for rolling or covering tubes)
- Scissors
- PVA glue
- Ready mixed or powder paint and brushes
- Stiff card (for a collage background)

What to do

Gather together a collection of cylinders. Include a range of heights and diameters by cutting ready made tubes into sections or rolling your own cylinders.

Decorating the cylinders: paint the cylinders with a mixture of paint and PVA glue. The thickened paint will provide a good covering for the cylinders, as well as a bright, glossy finish. Decorate with paint patterns, blobs of glitter glue, sequins, stickers, small flat buttons and so on. Alternatively, roll tubes from patterned paper or use the paper to cover ready made cylinders.

Making the collage: arrange the cylinders on a card background and stick them on lengthways with a line of PVA glue. Stick on short cylinders by putting a thick ring of glue on the paper and then placing the cylinder on top of the ring. Experiment with different backgrounds. Try sticking the cylinders onto a cork tile or a piece of wallpaper with an interesting pattern (*see BACKGROUNDS FOR COLLAGE box on page 71 for some more suggestions*). Choose a background to complement the colours of the cylinders. For example, brown, orange and yellow painted cylinders look effective against a cork tile.

Use for

Exploring 3-D shapes: introduce cylinder collage as part of a project on 3dimensional shapes.

Tree trunks: sponge paint tall tubes with shades of brown paint. Glue the cylinders lengthways to a card background and add crumpled green tissue to make foliage.

Robots: cover boxes and cylinders with silver foil and glue them onto a large sheet of card to make a robot. Use the boxes for the robot's body and head and make the arms and legs from cylinders. Add bottle tops and cut-out card to make the robot's features.

Robot by Joe (10)

Covering cylinders

Follow these steps to cover a cylinder with paper:

- Draw a rectangle on a sheet of paper (the height of the rectangle should be approximately 4cm taller than the height of the cylinder).
- Check that the rectangle is wide enough to go comfortably around the girth of the cylinder.
- Cut out the rectangle.
- Cover the cylinder with a thin layer of PVA glue.
- Roll the paper rectangle around the cylinder, leaving a margin of paper sticking above and below the ends of the cylinder.
- Snip the two margins of paper into a fringe.
- Spread glue around the inside ends of the cylinder and fold the fringe down inside so that it is firmly stuck.

Patterned papers for covering boxes and cylinders

Use wrapping paper to cover cylinders and boxes, or make your own patterned papers.

Try the following techniques:

- Lines of brush effects (*page 25*) • Patchwork pencil patterns (*page 12*)
- Wax rubbings (*page 50*) • Wax resist patterns (*page 52*) • Marbled paper (*page 39*)
- Bubble prints (*page 40*) • Torn strips of tissue paper (*page 82*)
- Raindrop tissue (*page 86*) • Textured paper (*page 33*) • Pierced paper (*page 75*)
- String block prints (*page 129*) • String tube prints (*page 130*)

Cylinder pencil holder (4+)

This handmade cylindrical pencil holder makes an appealing gift for men in the family.

You will need

- Card inner tubes from paper towels
- A shoe box lid
- Pencil and ruler
- Scissors
- Wrapping paper or home made decorative paper (*see PATTERNED PAPERS FOR COVERING BOXES AND CYLINDERS box above for some suggestions*)
- PVA glue

What to do

Cut the cylinders into different heights and cover with wrapping paper or decorative paper.

Cover the rim of the shoe box lid with strips of paper, leaving an overlap on the base and underneath of the lid.

Cut out a rectangle of paper, exactly the same size as the base of the lid.

Glue the rectangle to the base of the lid so that the entire lid is covered with paper (apart from the underneath).

Arrange the tubes into a group and use PVA glue to stick them firmly together down their sides.

Trail thick circles of PVA glue onto the box lid to attach the tubes (the glue will dry to a clear finish and won't show on the finished item).

Rest some small books on top of the tubes to hold them down as the glue dries.

Put pens and pencils in the cylinders. Use the tray for rubbers, notepads and other small stationery items.

Cylinder Father Christmas (4+)

A paper towel inner tube makes a good 'body' for this fun model of Father Christmas.

You will need

- The inner tube from a paper towel roll, cut to about two thirds of the original height.
- Red crêpe paper
- Lightweight card in black, brown and red
- Stiff card to make a base
- Newspaper
- Pink tissue paper
- Sticky tape
- White cotton wool
- PVA glue
- Scissors
- A hole puncher

What to do

Cover the card cylinder with red crêpe paper.

Glue a thin strip of brown paper around the middle of the cylinder to make a belt.

Make black card dots with a hole puncher and stick them onto the cylinder to represent buttons.

Glue small pieces of white cotton wool around the base of the cylinder.

Make a head by crumpling some newspaper into a ball.

Cut several sheets of pink tissue into circles, wrap them around the newspaper ball and secure the ends of the tissue with sticky tape.

Glue around the inside rim of the cylinder and rest the head on top.

Glue on a white cotton wool beard and two black dots to represent eyes.

Make a hat by folding a semi-circle of red card into a cone.

Glue small pieces of cotton wool on the point of the hat and around the bottom, and glue the hat to the head.

Cut out a small piece of stiff card to make a base.

Put a thick ring of PVA glue on the base and stick on the Father Christmas.

Use for

Father Christmas name place holder: cut out a long thin strip of red card. Glue it to the back of Father Christmas's body to represent arms. Write the name of a dinner guest on a small rectangle of paper and glue it to one of the arms.

Father Christmas sweet holder: make a sack for Father Christmas from a single egg box section, painted with a mixture of PVA glue and brown paint. Cut out a base from stiff card, large enough to accommodate both Father Christmas and his sack. Glue the model and the sack to the base and fill the sack with wrapped sweets or a small gift.

Some more cylindrical models

Abstract cylinder sculpture: cover several cylinders with decorative paper. Working on a base of stiff card, build the cylinders into a free standing abstract model.

Fairy castle: gather together cylinders of different sizes. Cap each one with a cone folded from a semicircle of paper. Paint the cylinders or cover with marbled paper (*see page 39*) and glue them together to make a fairy castle.

Palm trees: roll up a sheet of brown sugar paper. Tape the loose edge and cut a fringe into one end of the roll. Fold down the outer layers of the fringe to create the palm leaves and paint them green.

Chinese lanterns: decorate a rectangle of thin card with festive Chinese colours such as red and gold. Fold the rectangle in half and cut strips into the fold, leaving a margin of uncut paper. Open out the rectangle and roll it into a cylinder so that the cut strips are vertical. Tape the edge of the lantern, add a strip of card across the top to make a handle and tape on some silk tassels to dangle from the bottom.

Collage with boxes (3+)

As with cylinders, different sized boxes can be decorated and stuck onto a card background to make an attractive relief collage.

You will need

- A variety of small card boxes in different shapes and sizes
- Scissors
- PVA glue
- Paint and brushes
- Decorative papers (*see PATTERNED PAPERS FOR COVERING BOXES AND CYLINDERS box on page 68 for suggestions*)
- Stiff card (for a collage background)

What to do

Gather together a variety of small boxes such as containers for stock cubes, herbs, teabags and matchboxes. Challenge the children to help you find as many different boxes as possible. When you have completed your collection, cover the boxes with decorated paper or paint them with a mixture of ready mixed paint and PVA glue. The thickened glue should cover the glossy, patterned surfaces of the boxes. Once the paint is dry, arrange the boxes on a stiff card background and stick them on with PVA glue. Experiment with different backgrounds - see BACKGROUNDS FOR COLLAGE box below for some suggestions.

Use for

Exploring 3-D shapes: introduce collage with boxes as part of a project on 3-D shape. If possible, include cube shaped boxes as well as the more common cuboids. Add to the 3-D theme with card tubes (cylinders), ping pong or polystyrene balls (spheres), triangular chocolate boxes (rectangular prisms) and blown egg shells (ovoids).

Skyscraper collage: paint different sized boxes in greys, terracottas, browns and sandstones. Mix sand with the paint to give a textured effect. Alternatively, cover the boxes with patterned paper such as wax rubbings (*see page 50*). Cut out some small squares and rectangles from black paper and stick them on to represent the windows. Paint a sky background on a strip of paper and stick the boxes along the bottom of the paper to make a row of skyscrapers.

A greetings card: cover a small box with wrapping paper or decorative paper (*see PATTERNED PAPERS AND COVERING BOXES AND CYLINDERS box on page 68 for suggestions*). Add a bow made from coloured cellophane and a small, handmade gift tag with the recipient's name. Fold a piece of card in half and glue the 'gift' to the front of the card. Choose wrapping paper to fit in with the theme of the card – hearts and flowers for Mother's Day, an abstract or tartan pattern for Father's Day, Christmassy motifs for Christmas.

Backgrounds for collage

You can use just about anything to make a collage background:

- hessian • textured wallpaper • patterned wallpaper • corrugated card
- silver foil • felt • fabric •wood • cork tiles • painted polystyrene tiles
- sheets of coloured craft • foam • brown paper

Towers and totem poles (3.5+)

Boxes are the ideal scrap material for constructing model buildings. Decorate a range of boxes and challenge the children to build them into a tower or a totem pole.

You will need

- A variety of scrap boxes
- Paint and thick brushes
- PVA glue
- Decorative papers (*see PATTERNED PAPERS FOR COVERING BOXES AND CYLINDERS box on page 68 for suggestions*)
- Scissors

What to do

Towers: decorate the boxes, using paint with an added texture such as sand or oatmeal. You can also cover the boxes with an appropriate patterned paper such as wax rubbings (*see page 50*). Stick on black paper squares and rectangles to make windows. Arrange the boxes in order from largest to smallest and build them into a tower, using the largest box as a base. If necessary, stick the boxes together with dabs of PVA glue. Get the children to try different arrangements before sticking the boxes. What happens if they start off with the smallest box and build up to the largest box? Can they build up the tower with a random mixture of large and small boxes? Which effect do they prefer?

Totem poles: to make a totem pole, you will need boxes of roughly similar size and shape, for example tea boxes. If possible, have a look at some pictures of totem poles for inspiration. Use bright colours and bold patterns to decorate the boxes and paint a simple face onto one of the boxes. Build up the totem pole, occasionally positioning a box horizontally. Put the box with the face at the top. Because the boxes are all the same size, it is harder to balance a totem pole. If necessary, help the children with the construction.

Other things to make with boxes

- doll's houses • doll's house furniture • a vehicle • a treasure chest
- a decorated base for other models • a puppet theatre

Scrap models

Try recycling these for junk models:

- egg boxes • bubble wrap • polystyrene pieces • plastic water bottles • lolly sticks
- matchsticks • drinking straws • plastic ready meal containers • milk bottle tops

Textured paper collage (all ages)

Textured paper is a great collage material. Even the simplest collage picture is effective because the colours, textures and patterns of the paper are attractive in themselves.

You will need

- A variety of textured papers, such as corrugated paper and handmade paper, woven paper, parchment, textured wallpaper, woodchip paper (anaglypta), stippled pastel paper (Ingres paper), watercolour paper
- A stiff card background
- PVA glue
- Scissors
- Ready mixed paint, sponge, wax crayon and chalks (optional)

What to do

Use a variety of textured papers to make a collage picture. Encourage the children to keep their pictures simple, to show off the different textures and subtle patterns of the paper. Experiment with cutting and tearing the paper into strips and shapes. Colour the paper by sponging a small amount of paint across the paper, or rubbing with the side of a wax crayon or stick of chalk. The aim is to add colour without 'drowning' the texture.

Use for

Abstract collage: cut out or tear strips and shapes from different textured papers. Arrange the shapes into an abstract collage, showing off the interesting textures, patterns and colours of the different papers.

A textured paper patchwork mount: cut out squares of different textured papers. Glue them onto a large sheet of card to create a patchwork and use as a mount for small, flat items such as pressed flowers, leaves, feathers, crystals, fossils, shells, photos, drawings, prints and individual wax rubbings. Glue a single item to each square of paper.

Patchwork fields: use a sponge to dab green and brown paint onto different types of textured paper. Cut the paper into squares and rectangles and stick them onto a background to make a patchwork of fields. Use brown corrugated paper or card for ploughed fields. Make trees and bushes from pressed leaves or crumpled tissue paper.

Animal skins: use robust handmade paper, textured wallpaper or woodchip paper to make the rough skin for collage animals such as reptiles and dinosaurs.

Textured paper rubbings and prints

Create a textured paper collage and use it to make wax crayon rubbings and prints. Make sure that all the textured surfaces are as level with each other as possible - otherwise, not all of the picture will show up on the rubbing / print. Take the wax

crayon rubbing before covering the picture with paint. Once painted put paper on the collage to make a print. Roll across the paper with a rolling pin to ensure that all parts of the picture are pressed down. Compare the rubbing and the print. Can the children see that they have come from the same collage picture? Which effect do they prefer?

Creating textured paper (4+)

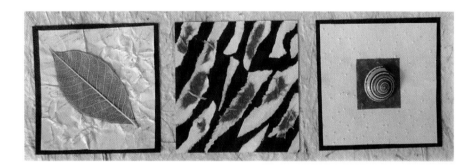

Although it is easy to collect all kinds of ready made textured papers, it is also fun to make your own.

You will need

- Cartridge paper
- Sugar paper
- Tissue paper
- Thin felt-tipped pens
- A folded towel
- Masking tape
- Tools for piercing, such as large darning needles or thin knitting needles
- Tea or coffee solution in a pudding bowl
- Coloured chalk

What to do

Try the following techniques to create different textured papers.

Tearing: tearing a strip from a sheet of paper results in an interesting textured edge. To tear a straight edge, place a heavy book on a sheet of cartridge or sugar paper. Leave a small margin of paper sticking out from under the book. Press down as hard as possible on the book and tear off the margin to make a torn paper strip. Move the book sideways and repeat the process. Use different colours and types of paper and stick the torn strips in overlapping rows to create some interesting textures.

Crumpling: crumple up a sheet of thin cartridge paper and then smooth it out to reveal an interesting creased texture. The more you crumple, the finer the creases and the softer the paper becomes. Experiment with crumpling different types of paper.

Staining crumpled paper: add colour by soaking a crumpled ball of paper in cold tea or coffee for a couple of minutes. Leave the ball to dry and then open it out. The creases will have absorbed more of the colour, giving the paper a crackled, batik-like effect.

Chalking crumpled paper: rub the side of a stick of coloured chalk across a sheet of creased paper. Press lightly so that the chalk only colours the raised creases. The results are surprisingly effective.

Piercing: place a sheet of cartridge paper on a towel or piece of felt. Pierce holes in the paper with a darning needle or a thin knitting needle. Using a felt pen, draw a pattern onto very thin paper, such as tissue. Tape the tissue onto the cartridge paper and pierce out the pattern so that the holes go through the tissue paper to the cartridge paper beneath.

> **Tip**
> *When tearing paper, make sure you work with the grain. It is much harder to tear across the grain, and the effect will be more ragged and uneven.*

Use for

Free collage: encourage the children to make different textures and use them in their free collage.

Picture mounts: make an interesting mount for a small picture by layering several textured papers, one on top of the other. Start off with a large sheet of crumpled paper. Add a slightly smaller sheet with a pierced border. Add a smaller sheet with a border of torn edges. You can also add one or two layers of ready made paper, such as a textured wallpaper or handmade paper. A large layered mount of this type sets off a simple picture such as a textured paper print or a pierced paper design.

A homemade textured paper sampler: show off your home made textured papers by turning them into a decorative wallhanging. Make as many different samples as possible and mount them on a large sheet of paper to form a patchwork. The patchwork can also be used to display small objects or pictures (*see Textured paper collage / A textured paper patchwork mount, page 73 for some suggestions*).

Ancient maps (6+): smooth out a sheet of crumpled paper that has been stained with coffee (*see Staining crumpled paper, above*), and use it to make an ancient treasure map. Draw paths, crosses and other markings with thin felt pens.

Tearing strips

Tearing strips of paper is easier with two children. Get one child to lean heavily on the book while the other tears.

Paper folding (5+)

'Folding' is yet another technique that can be used to create handmade textures in an ordinary sheet of paper.

You will need

- Cartridge paper
- Sugar paper
- Pencils

What to do

Try these ways of folding paper to create different textures and relief patterns.

Challenge the children to come up with some more ideas.

Folds: draw some faint pencil lines down a sheet of paper, approximately 1 to 2 centimetres apart. Place the paper flat on the table and fold along the lines, working backwards and forwards to create a zig-zag of folds. Pinch the folds at one end and secure with clear sticky tape to make a fan. Alternatively, you can pinch the fan at the centre and secure it with tape so that the folds splay out at both ends.

Zig-zags: fold strips of sturdy paper into zig-zags and stick them onto a card background. Spread a layer of PVA glue across the paper and stick on the entire length of the zig-zag. Alternatively, glue on one end of the zig-zag so that it 'springs' out of the paper.

Crinkly chips: start off with two long rectangles of paper in different colours, for example blue and red. Fold each rectangle two or three times to make thin strips. Place the ends of the strips at right angles to each other, so that the blue end is on top of the red end. Fold the red strip across the end of the blue strip. Fold the blue strip across the end of the red strip. Continue until both strips are completely intertwined to create a colourful 'crinkly chip'.

Quilling (7+): quilling is a traditional craft that involves rolling long strips of card into spirals and sticking them horizontally onto a background. Cut out several strips of lightweight coloured card, approximately half a centimetre wide and 10cm long. Show the children how to roll the strips around a pencil to make spirals. Put a thick layer of PVA glue on a stiff card background and stick on the spirals. Don't worry if the spirals loosen a little during the gluing process – they often make more interesting shapes when they are not so tightly coiled. Challenge nimble fingered children to make straight sided and oval spirals. Vary the effect by rolling a short strip to make a small spiral and a long strip to make a fat spiral. Try coiling two different coloured strips to make a variegated spiral.

Use for

Decorated fans: fans were traditionally decorated with feathers, lace and silk tassels. Glue strips of lace along the top of the paper rectangle before folding it into a fan. Stick

a feather to the top of each fold and tape a silk tassel to the 'handle'. Use the fans to cool yourself down on a hot day.

'Pop up' greetings cards: fold a short strip of sturdy paper into a zig-zag. Tape one end of the zig-zag to a cut-out card motif. Tape the other end to the front of a greetings card, so that the motif stands out from the card.

Wriggly creatures: zig-zags and 'crinkly chips' can be turned into caterpillars and other wriggly creatures. Decorate the strip of card before folding it into a zig-zag and use a green strip and a yellow strip to make a 'crinkly chip' caterpillar.

Paper beads (6+)

Rolling paper strips and triangles to make beads is quite simple to do, once you get the hang of it. The beads can either be turned into jewellery or used for collage and other projects.

You will need

- White and coloured copier paper
- Scissors
- PVA glue
- A knitting needle
- Plasticine
- Thin felt-tipped pens, including gold
- Ribbon or cord

What to do

Single strip beads: cut out a long thin strip of paper. The width of the strip will determine the width of the finished bead. The length of the strip will determine how fat the finished bead becomes. Decorate one side of the strip with small patterns such as squiggles, dots or tiny stars. Rest the knitting needle between two lumps of Plasticine. Spread a thin layer of PVA glue across the back of the patterned strip and roll it tightly around the knitting needle. When the whole strip has been rolled, secure the end with more PVA glue. Leave the glue to dry and then slide the bead off the knitting needle.

Double strip beads: cut out two long thin triangles of paper in contrasting colours. One triangle should be slightly thinner than the other. Stick the two triangles together with PVA glue so that the wider triangle creates a margin of colour around the thinner triangle. The margin should be no wider than 2mm. Roll the triangles around the knitting needle, starting with the base of the triangles and finishing with the point. The resulting bead should have an attractive variegated look.

Use for

Necklaces: thread the beads onto thin ribbon or cord to create a necklace. Make different sized beads and choose colours and patterns that go together. Combine paper

beads with other handmade beads such as clay beads or marbled fimo beads.

Bracelets and anklets: thread two or three beads onto thin elastic to make a bracelet or anklet.

Collage: use colourful beads to decorate an abstract collage, or roll beads from natural coloured papers and use to make the bodies of birds and insects.

Hangings and mobiles: thread paper beads onto lengths of coloured wool. Wind ribbon around a wire coat hanger and tie on the bead hangings to make a mobile (*see also Shell hangings, page 146 and Dream catchers, page 135*).

Paper cutting (5+)

Cutting paper into different shapes and patterns is yet another way of creating textures.

You will need

- Cartridge paper
- Coloured copier paper
- Pencil
- Scissors

What to do

Once children are competent with using scissors, try the following techniques:

Paper slits: use cartridge paper or thin card for this activity. Fold a sheet of paper in half. Snip two sides of a small triangle into the fold. Open up the paper and fold back each of the four little triangles to create a raised pattern. Snip a row of triangles, open out the paper and fold back the left and right triangles for the first cut, the top and bottom triangles for the next cut and all four triangles for the third cut. Continue along the row to create a pattern. Rub over the back of the paper with a wax crayon, before cutting out the triangles. When you fold back the triangles, their contrasting colour will add to the textured relief effect.

Spirals: cut out a circle of coloured paper. Using a pencil, draw a faint spiral line from the centre of the circle to the outside edge. Cut out the spiral and stick just the one end to a background so that the spiral dangles freely.

Paper chains: fold a rectangle of paper back and forth to create a concertina. Draw a picture on the top fold of paper, making sure that a part of the picture is drawn against the fold. Cut out the picture and open up the folds to reveal a chain of identical shapes.

Paper lace: fold a square or a circle of paper into quarters. Snip small triangles and squares into the edges of the folded paper. Open up the paper to reveal a symmetrical lacy pattern.

Use for

Decorative borders and frames: use triangular paper slits to decorate the borders of mounting paper. Make strips of paper decorated with slits and glue them onto a cardboard picture frame.

Pig's tail: a spiral cut from thin pink card makes a good tail for a collage or model pig (*see Papier mâché balloons / Pigs, page 98*).

Snakes: draw a pencil spiral on both sides of a thin card circle and decorate each side with snake-like patterns. Cut out the spiral and draw on two pen dots for eyes and stick on a forked tongue cut from thin red card. Glue one end of the snake to a rainforest collage picture, or dangle the snakes from a ribbon covered wire coat hanger to make a mobile.

A friendship frieze: cut out a chain of people shapes, all holding hands. Paint the faces with 'people colours' (*see page 24*) or stick on small portrait photographs to create a friendship frieze.

Christmas garlands: cut out paper chains of holly leaves, stars or Christmas trees. Paint the shapes and decorate with glitter and sequins.

Birthday garlands: make a special birthday frieze by cutting out a chain of birthday cake shapes. Paint the shapes and write 'happy birthday to ...' in large letters across the cakes.

Paper lace window decorations: cut out a paper lace pattern from black paper and stick coloured cellophane or tissue across the holes to make a window decoration (*see Cellophane stained glass / Medieval rose windows, page 89*).

Card and paper weaving (4.5+)

Weaving with strips of card or paper is simple but effective. Use plain coloured card or patterned paper.

You will need

- At least two different colours or patterns of paper
- Scissors
- A craft knife, wooden board and metal ruler (*for adult use only – see USING A CRAFT KNIFE box on page 90*)

What to do

Make a 'warp' (upright) frame of strips by folding a square of paper in half and cutting evenly spaced lines into the fold. Leave a margin of uncut paper at the opposite end to the fold. Open out the paper and weave thin strips of paper (the 'weft') in and out of the warp.

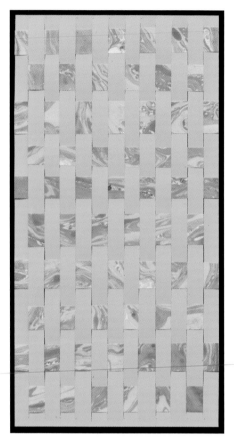

Experiment with the following ideas:

• Weave together different combinations of colour and pattern.
• Cut the warp frame so that the strips are different widths.
• Cut the weft strips into different widths.
• Cut the weft strips into different lengths and leave them overlapping the edges of the warp frame.
• Try weaving torn weft strips through the warp frame.
• Cut out different shapes to make into a warp frame – for example, a circle, a diamond, a heart, a leaf, an irregular shape.
• Use a craft knife and metal ruler to cut slots in the paper and weave thin strips through the slots.

Paper weaving

Use for

A gift bag: make two separate weavings. Glue one weaving onto each side of a sturdy paper bag with handles to create an attractive gift bag.

A mat: use a sturdy card weaving as a table mat for an ornament.

Mounts and backgrounds: weave together strips of naturally coloured papers and use as a mount for a simple picture or as a background for collage.

Some more weaving activities

Just about any long thin item can be turned into a weaving. For some other types of weaving, see the following:

• Nature weaving (*page 118*)
• Fabric weaving (*page 123*)
• Weaving with 'stringy things' (*page 132*)

Chapter 5

Tissue paper, cellophane and silver foil

About tissue paper

Tissue paper has a delicate, translucent quality which can be built up in layers to produce shades of colour. It can also be pasted over strongly coloured card or paper shapes to create a misty effect. Because it is so delicate, it is easy to tear. This means that even young children can create torn collage pieces. But the lightweight quality of tissue paper can make it difficult to handle – it's not always suitable for the under four age group.

Thanks to its special qualities, many of the most interesting tissue paper effects are created by accident. Tissue quickly becomes wrinkly with glue and the colours will tend to 'bleed' into each other when the paper gets wet. Far from being a problem, this can add all kinds of exciting textures and patterns to a tissue paper collage. Only some tissue papers are colourfast. For the tissue paper painting (*see page 86*), you need to make sure that you have the right type of tissue paper.

For some projects, you may find that the sturdier crêpe paper is a better choice than tissue paper. Like tissue, crêpe paper has a thin, lightweight quality that makes it good for covering objects - without the risk of it tearing or disintegrating when wet. Use it for wrapping around cardboard boxes and tubes as part of a sculpture.

About cellophane

Cellophane has a glowing, glass-like quality that makes it useful for creating shiny collage effects. It is even more translucent than tissue paper and makes wonderful stained glass panels. It comes in all colours of the rainbow, although the warm colours (reds, yellows and oranges) tend to be more striking than the cold colours (blues and greens). Colourless cellophane is particularly useful for simulating windows and making pocket-like containers to display small items of interest. Like tissue paper, it is cheap and easily available from art and craft shops, stationers and schools suppliers. It usually comes in large rolls, although you can buy it in sheets. It is also possible to buy shredded cellophane - a tangled bundle of thin strips, useful for creating all sorts of collage effects.

About silver foil

Apart from its beautiful shiny silver appearance, silver foil makes a versatile collage medium. As well as using it in its smooth state or crumpling it to create a texture, children can mould it into different shapes. It's for any collages or models with a 'space' or 'machine' theme.

Silver foil is cheap and easily available and you can recycle used pieces from the kitchen (carefully washed, of course). Use other scrap foil items too, such as milk bottle tops or aluminium takeaway containers.

Activities

Tissue paper collage (4+)

The delicate, translucent quality of tissue paper makes it easy to crumple, tear and build up into shaded layers.

You will need

• Different coloured tissue paper
• Card
• Scissors
• PVA glue

What to do

Tissue paper layers: cut out several pieces of tissue paper in a single colour. Glue the pieces onto a thin card background, overlapping them to create shades of colour. The more layers you have, the stronger the colour. Experiment with combining two different colours and watch how the glue changes the appearance of the tissue.

Tissue paper overlay: glue a piece of light coloured tissue, such as white or pale blue, on top of a strongly coloured card shape. Once the glue has dried, the shape and colour of the card will show through the translucent tissue, creating an unusual effect.

Crumpling: crumple large pieces of tissue into balls and then smooth them out to create an attractive creased texture. Glue them onto card with PVA glue.

Torn strips: because tissue paper tears so easily, a torn edged shape tends to be more visually interesting than a cut edged shape. Try tearing tissue paper into strips and sticking them onto a contrasting card background, to show off the torn edges. Experiment with leaving the end of the tissue strip unstuck so that it hangs free of the background.

Tissue paper, cellophane and silver foil

. . . .

Use for

Landscapes and seascapes: torn strips of tissue can be built up in layers to create landscape and seascape backgrounds. Try strips of yellow and orange for sand, shades of blue for sea and sky and greens and browns for fields.

Mist: use the tissue paper overlay technique to create mist. Make a collage picture of trees and houses using strongly coloured card or paper. Spread a thin layer of PVA glue over the picture and carefully press a sheet of white tissue onto the glue. As the glue dries, the shapes will show through the tissue, looking as if they are swathed in a white mist.

Tissue paper relief collage (4+)

Because tissue paper is so thin, it can easily be twisted, crumpled and rolled into balls to create a textured relief collage.

You will need

- Sheets of tissue paper
- Small containers
- Scissors
- Thin card
- PVA glue
- Jar of clean water and brushes

What to do

Tissue paper balls: crumple lots of small pieces of tissue paper into tight balls. Store the balls in separate containers, sorted according to colour.

Tissue paper clumps: crumple large pieces of tissue into loose balls. Stick them on carefully so that they do not come loose.

Twisted strips: cut a sheet of tissue into strips and twist the strips into tight strings. Try twisting two contrasting colours together.

Moulded tissue: if you use lots of glue, the tissue paper will quickly turn soggy. Spread plenty of PVA glue on a sheet of card and stick on a piece of tissue. Add more glue and pieces of tissue, building up the layers. As the tissue paper becomes soggy with glue, mould it into ridges and bumps.

Use for

Tissue ball mosaic: working on card, create a pencil drawing made up of large, simple shapes. Cover one shape at a time with a layer of PVA glue and stick on the tissue paper balls, making sure that the balls are tightly packed together. This can be quite fiddly and time consuming so make it a shared project. To prevent children from losing patience, keep designs small and help rolling up the balls.

. . . .

Trees and foliage: tight tissue balls and loosely crumpled pieces of tissue can be used to represent bushes or the foliage of trees. Twist strips of brown tissue to make trunks, twigs and branches.

Crowns and masks: use tissue paper balls to make jewels for crowns. Use twisted strips, balls and moulded tissue to make eyebrows, beards and other features on masks.

Tissue paper flowers (6+)

The delicate texture and bright colours of tissue make it the perfect material for constructing paper flowers.

You will need

- Tissue paper
- PVA glue
- Clear sticky tape
- Scissors

What to do

Circular blooms: cut out a series of three or four tissue paper circles, ranging from large to small. Put a small dot of glue in the centre of the largest circle and stick on the next largest circle. Continue until the tissue paper circles form a pile, all stuck together at their centres. Grip the centre of the largest circle at the back. Pinch it into a point so that the circles bunch together to form the flower. Wrap a small piece of sticky tape around the point to make a short 'stalk'. Experiment with different combinations of colour. Create a centre for the flower by using a contrasting colour for the smallest circle.

Buds: cut out a long strip of tissue paper, slightly thinner at one end to form a wedge shaped triangle. Starting at the thinner end of the triangle, roll it up loosely to form a bud that is just starting to unfurl. As you roll, pinch the bottom of the bud to create a short 'stalk'. Wrap a small piece of sticky tape around the stalk to hold it secure. As with circular blooms, experiment with different colours. Try rolling up two different coloured strips to create a 'variegated' bud.

> **Tip**
> *Tissue paper flowers can be quite fiddly. Younger children can make flowers by loosely crumpling a piece of tissue and sticking it onto a background.*

Use for

Spring blossom: combine white and pink circles to make Spring blossom. Tie the blossoms to real twigs (*see Twig trees, page 154*) or stick onto a sponge painted tree trunk. For an authentic look, cut out the trunk and branches from brown wax bark rubbings (*see page 50*).

Jungles and rainforests: make tropical blooms from brightly coloured tissue paper such as yellows, oranges and reds. Stick them onto a rainforest background.

Decorating hats: tissue paper flowers are useful for decorating hats, particularly Easter bonnets. Fold a strip of card into a circlet and tape on tissue blooms and buds. Use Spring-like colours, such as pale green, yellow and pink.

Greetings cards: stick white and pink tissue paper blossoms onto a pale pink or green background to make a pretty Easter card. For a Valentine's Day card, use bright red tissue to make red roses. For a Mother's Day card, let the children make flowers using their mother's favourite colours.

Cling film tissue collage (6+)

Make a collage without a background by gluing tissue paper onto cling film. The collage can then be taped onto a window to show off the delicate, translucent colours of the tissue.

You will need

- A sheet of cling film, preferably the tough variety designed for the freezer
- Tissue paper (colourfast)
- PVA glue
- A thick brush

What to do

Spread out the cling film so that it is lying flat on the table. Arrange some torn pieces and strips of tissue paper on top of the cling film. Thin down the PVA glue with water and brush it over the tissue shapes. Arrange more pieces on top of the first layer, making sure that some of the pieces overlap. Brush over with glue. Continue building up the layers. When the collage is finished, leave it to dry. Once the glue is completely dry, carefully peel the tissue away from the cling film. Tape the collage against a window pane.

> **Tip**
> *Cling film tissue collage is much more effective if the tissue doesn't bleed its colour when wet. Check that your tissue paper is colourfast for this project.*

Use for

Underwater scenes: start off with a layer of pale blue tissue made up of torn pieces. Add some brightly coloured 'fish' shapes and strips of green to represent seaweed. Partly cover the fish with torn strips of pale blue to make it look as though they are swimming underwater.

Christmas window decorations: cut out some simple Christmassy shapes such as an angel, a Christmas tree, a circle to represent a bauble or a square to represent

a wrapped present. Build up layers of tissue paper and glue, including some small pieces of brightly coloured tissue as decorations. When the shapes are dry, peel off the clingfilm. Punch a hole in the top of the shape, thread gift ribbon through the hole and hang from a window.

Tissue paper painting (3+)

As long as you use tissue paper designed to 'bleed' its colour when wet, you can create some interesting effects by adding water to a tissue paper collage.

You will need

- Non-colourfast tissue paper
- Watercolour or sturdy cartridge paper
- Scissors
- A jar of clean water
- A sponge
- Thick brushes

What to do

'Glued shape' painting: tear or cut the tissue paper into shapes. Using small dabs of PVA glue, stick the shapes onto the paper. Brush over the shapes with clean water so that the colours start to bleed into the wet surface of the paper. Experiment with the amount of water you need and try layering shapes and combining colours.

'Peeled shape' painting: using a strong colour such as red, tear or cut some tissue paper into shapes. Wash over a sheet of white cartridge paper with a damp sponge and lay the tissue shapes on the surface. Gently brush over the shapes with a wet brush and leave the paper to dry. As the tissue paper starts to peel at the edges, lift it off to reveal the transferred coloured shapes beneath.

'Raindrop' tissue: create a raindrop effect by dripping clean water onto a sheet of tissue. The drops of water will leach the colour out of the tissue, making it look as though it has been studded with raindrops or tears.

> ### Tip
> *Not all tissue stains the background paper strongly enough for the 'peeled shape' painting activity to be effective. Before trying it with children, have a quick experiment to check which colours to use. If none of your colours are strong enough, stick with the 'glued shape' approach.*

Use for

Underwater fish: cut out fish shapes from blue and green tissue. Use small blobs of PVA glue to stick them onto the paper. Wash over the shapes with clean water and a thick

brush. Some of the colour will bleed from the tissue to create a watery surrounding for the fish. Add other watery features, such as cut-out bubble prints (*see page 40*).

Butterflies: cut out butterfly shapes from different coloured tissue. Using either the 'glued shape' or the 'peeled shape' approach, wash over the tissue with clean water. When the butterflies are dry, decorate their wings with gold and silver pens.

Butterflies by Hannah (11)

Poppies: cut out poppy shapes from red tissue. If the tissue stains the paper strongly enough, use the 'peeled shape' approach. If not, stick on the tissue shapes with PVA glue. Dab around the poppies to create a misty red halo. When dry, use dabs of black paint or a black felt pen to draw in the centres of the flowers.

Rainy day backgrounds: use a sheet of blue raindrop tissue as the background for a rainy picture. Stick on large raindrops cut from pale blue card and add some grey thunder clouds made from sprayed paint (*see page 28*).

Cellophane collage (all ages)

Like tissue paper, cellophane can be used in a number of different ways to create collage effects.

You will need

- Cellophane
- Shredded cellophane
- Glue
- Scissors
- Card for a background

What to do

Start by choosing the colour of the background. You may find that brilliant white card is the best.

Layering cellophane: show the children how to overlap pieces of cellophane to create darker shades and new colours.

Cellophane overlay: stick translucent sheets of cellophane over cut-out card shapes.

Crumpled cellophane: create texture by gluing crumpled cellophane to a background.

Shredded cellophane: stick on shredded cellophane in tangled clumps. Separate out some of the strands and use just two or three.

Use for

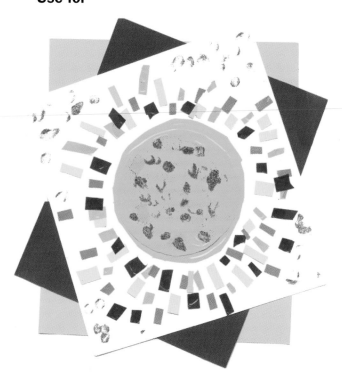

Cellophane Sunrise by Ellie (8)

Sunbursts: the shiny, translucent qualities of cellophane make it an effective material for collage sunsets and sunrises. Cut out a large yellow paper circle and stick it onto the centre of a pale blue card background. Cover the circle with a larger circle of yellow cellophane. Cut out thin strips of yellow, red and orange card and arrange them around the circle to represent the sun's rays. Intersperse with strips of yellow, red and orange cellophane.

Flames: combine yellow, orange and red card flame shapes with flames cut from cellophane.

Crazy hair: draw or paint faces and stick them onto a card background. Glue shredded cellophane around the face to represent hair.

Cellophane stained glass (7+)

The translucent quality of the cellophane gives a sophisticated finish to a 'stained glass window' collage. Working on black card or paper adds a traditional leaded appearance to the cellophane 'glass'.

You will need

- White paper, pencils and felt-tipped pens for designs
- Black marker pens
- Black card and black paper
- White pencils or chalk
- Sheets of different coloured cellophane
- A craft or Stanley knife, wooden board, masking tape and metal ruler (for adult use only)

What to do

Designing the window: start by making designs for the stained glass windows. Give the children pencils, felt-tipped pens and sheets of paper cut to the same size and shape as the black card. Emphasise that the design should be made up of simple shapes and that each shape should have a thick black outline. Have a look at pictures of stained glass windows and show the children how each shape is outlined with lead. Provide black marker pens so that they can draw in the 'lead' outlines on their practice designs.

Making the window: ask each child to draw their design on a piece of black card, using a white pencil or chalk. Check that the design has been correctly transferred. Place the card on a wooden board and use a craft knife to cut out the shapes, leaving window-like holes in the card (see USING A CRAFT KNIFE box, page 90). If necessary, secure the card to the board with masking tape before starting to cut. For straight lines, cut along a metal ruler. NB only adults should use a craft knife.

Adding the 'glass': glue small pieces of different coloured cellophane across the back of each cut-out hole. Cut each piece so that it is only just larger than the hole, otherwise you may get edges of cellophane overlapping an adjacent hole. Tape the finished collage to the window so that the sunlight makes the cellophane colours glow.

> **Tip**
> *To make small round holes in the card, use a hole puncher. Stick small pieces of coloured cellophane behind each hole.*

Use for

Medieval rose windows: medieval rose windows are circular and divided into segments. To make a rose window, fold a circle of black paper into quarters and cut triangles out of each edge (see Paper cutting / Paper lace, page 78 and Paper lace window decorations, page 79). Open out the circle and stick coloured cellophane behind each hole.

Using a craft knife

Craft knives are ideal for cutting out a shape within a piece of card - for example, projects such as cellophane stained glass. The knives are very sharp and should only be used by adults. Always work on a wooden chopping board and use masking tape to attach the card to the board. For straight lines, cut against the edge of a metal ruler as the blade will slice into wood or plastic.

Friendship windows (4+)

Colourless cellophane is completely see-through. This makes it the perfect 'glass' for making a collage window.

You will need

- Clear cellophane
- Scissors
- Thin card
- PVA glue
- Four or six small photos or drawings of friends and family, to stick behind the window glass

What to do

Cut a piece of pale coloured card into a window shape - round, square, rectangular or arched.

Using a ruler and pencil, divide the card into four or six equal sections.

Glue one picture of a friend or family member onto each section of the card.

Cut a piece of clear cellophane to the same shape and size as the card.

Put tiny dabs of PVA glue around the edges of the card shape.

Carefully stick the cellophane to the card so that just the edges are attached.

Choose a darker coloured card and cut it into thin strips.

Stick the strips horizontally and vertically across the middle of the cellophane so that one friend is peeping out of each pane.

Stick more strips around the edges to make window frames.

Tip

The card can be left plain or decorated with a pattern. Use pale colours to decorate the background card and darker colours to decorate the window frames. Choose from the following decorative techniques:
- *Brush effects (page 25)* • *Marbling (page 39)*
- *Prints (page 40)* • *Wax crayon effects (page 47)*
- *Wax rubbings (page 50)* • *Textured paper (page 74)* • *Tissue Paper (page 82)*

Cellophane wrappings

Use clear cellophane to wrap small, colourful sweets such as jelly beans. Stick them onto cut-out card shapes and use them as edible decorations for the Christmas tree.

Cellophane window greetings cards (6+)

Stuff a clear cellophane window with shredded cellophane to make this unusual greetings card.

You will need

- Clear cellophane
- Coloured shredded cellophane
- Coloured card, in a colour to complement the colour of the shredded cellophane
- Scissors
- Craft knife, wooden board and metal ruler (for adult use only)
- PVA glue

What to do

Cut the card into two rectangles so that the one piece of card (card A) is exactly half the width of the other piece of card (card B).

Draw a shape on card A and cut it out, using the craft knife, metal ruler and wooden board (only adults should use a craft knife).

Fold card B in half and place card A on top of card B.

Using the window in card A as a template, draw an identical pencil shape on card B. Glue clumps of shredded cellophane within the pencil shape on card B (don't worry if the strands of cellophane overlap the pencil lines – they will be hidden by card A).

Put small dabs of glue around the edge of the window in card A and stick a piece of clear cellophane across the back of the hole to make 'glass'.

Spread glue over the back of card A and place it over card B so that the cellophane window covers the shredded cellophane.

Gently press down on the edges of the window to ensure that the shredded cellophane is sealed within the window.

Decorate around the window with sequins, stickers, glitter or any other items of your choice.

Use for

Valentine's Day card: make a heart shaped template: fold a piece of card in half and draw one half of a heart shape against the fold; cut out the drawing and open up the card to reveal a symmetrical heart shaped template. Using the template, make a heart shaped cellophane window card. Fill the window with red, pink or pearlescent shredded cellophane.

Christmas card: cut out a triangular tree shaped window. Fill it with green or gold shredded cellophane and stick glitter and sequins around the tree.

Mother's Day card: cut out a simple flower shaped window and fill it with pink shredded cellophane or dried pot pourri.

Decorative items for cellophane pockets

Cellophane windows can be used to display lots of other small items.
Try the following:

• Small dried flower heads • Lavender • Pot pourri • Tiny shells
• Tiny pebbles • Ribbons • Small buttons • Small glass 'seed' beads
• Small, flat crystals • Scraps of lace • Sequins

Glue the items to the card background, before placing the cellophane window on top.

Silver foil collage (all ages)

As with tissue and cellophane, silver foil can be used in many different ways to create some interesting collage effects.

You will need

• Silver aluminium foil
• Other foil and metallic resources (see MORE METALLIC RESOURCES box, page 93)
• Scissors
• PVA glue
• Card (for a background)
• Ready mixed paint and brushes (optional – see PAINTING SILVER FOIL box, page 94)

What to do

Dark coloured card makes a good background for the shiny silver foil. Try the following techniques:

Tissue paper, cellophane and silver foil

Silver Foil Triptych by Viraj (3), Elsie (3) and Kian (3)

Foil shapes: cut or tear a flat sheet of foil into different shapes. Point out that the foil is shiny in one side and dull on the other. Introduce contrast to a collage by sticking on both shiny and dull shapes. Handle the shapes carefully as foil tears quite easily.

Foil balls: roll small pieces of foil into balls. Flatten the bases slightly by pressing them against the table – this makes them easier to stick onto a card background.

Crumpled foil: loosely crumple pieces of foil. Smooth out the foil to create flat shapes with an interesting creased texture. Alternatively, flatten the base of the shape and glue it onto the card background in its crumpled form.

Stamped foil: crumple up a large piece of foil and stamp on it several times to create a flat, wrinkly pancake.

Foil relief: sculpt the foil into different shapes and forms. Make the shapes easier to stick by flattening the bases.

Tip

Bearing hygiene in mind, wear slippers or indoor gym shoes when stamping on foil to make pancakes.

Some more metallic resources

- Milk bottle tops • Foil cake and tart containers • Foil takeaway containers
- Chocolate and sweet wrappers • Gold and silver paper • Gold and silver pens
- Metallic wax crayons • Metallic water based paint • Gold and silver glitter
- Gold and silver sticky stars and sequins • Small, shiny nuts and screws

Use for collages and models of robots, angels, spaceships, planes, machines and vehicles.

Silver foil plaques (4+)

Silver foil can be moulded over objects with interesting shapes to make an unusual plaque.

Spaghetti covered with foil

You will need

- Flattish objects with interesting shapes, such as an old pair of scissors, large safety pins, old combs, strands of spaghetti.
- A square of stiff card
- PVA glue
- A sheet of silver foil
- Ready mixed paint and brushes (optional – *see PAINTING SILVER FOIL box below*)

What to do

Arrange the items on a square of card, leaving a good space between each item. Encourage the children to try different arrangements until they are happy with their composition. Glue the items to the card and put a few blobs of glue on the card itself. Lay a sheet of silver foil over the card and carefully mould the foil around the items. Press and smooth the foil so that the shapes and details show through. The plaque can then be painted or left as it is.

Tip
Have a run through to check that a particular item is flat enough to be covered in foil, without the foil tearing. If in doubt, use very flat items such as spaghetti, safety pins and combs.

Painting silver foil

Silver foil can be painted using ready mixed paint blended with PVA glue. Brush on the paint and then wipe some of it from the surface of the foil so that the shiny silver texture shows through. This creates an attractive antiqued effect, particularly if you use black, brown or water based metallic paints such as gold, bronze or copper.

Chapter 6

Newspaper, magazines, wrapping paper and greetings cards

About newspaper

Turning old newspaper into beautiful artwork is a great way of recycling. The classic craft activity of papier mâché is one of the most obvious uses. As a variation, newspaper can also be turned into paper pulp which is more malleable. It can be moulded into relief shapes and used to decorate items such as masks, boxes or picture frames. It is also good for making effective collages. Tear it into different shapes, crumple it up or turn it into an unusual mount for black and white drawings. It can also be incorporated into mixed media pictures, try combining it with wax crayons, chalk and paint.

Use bold strokes and bright primary colours to contrast with the delicate black and white print.

About magazines

Magazines provide an endless source of pictures, patterns and motifs. You can find relevant magazine pictures for whatever topic you want to explore. The pages are often glossy, adding an attractive sheen to the artwork. The pictures can be cut into separate images and used for a 'realistic' collage, or you can cut out squares of colour and random shapes for mosaics or abstract pictures. Whenever you find an interesting page or image, tear it out and add it to your image bank.

About wrapping paper and greetings cards

Wrapping paper and greetings cards offer an endless supply of attractive motifs, pictures and patterns. Pictures cut from greetings cards can be used as a sticking activity for the under fours. The stiff texture makes them easy to handle and it's easy to find images children will like! The thinner texture of wrapping paper makes it a little more difficult to handle but it's useful for covering items, either as a single sheet or in the form of découpage (*see Wrapping paper découpage, page 103*). You can also look out for

wrapping paper designs to suit the purpose of the project – flowers for a découpage Mother's Day gift box; an abstract pattern to make a pen holder for dad; Christmas motifs for gift tags or cartoon characters to make a personalised birthday card for a child.

Newspaper is great for collage because ...

- You can tear it, crumple it up, paint it or cut it into separate words and shapes.
- The newsprint adds a delicate black and white pattern.
- It makes an effective mount for a monochrome drawing.
- It's good to reuse it, rather than throw it away.

Magazines are great for collage because ...

- You can cut out pictures of anything and everything.
- You can find lots of different colours and shades.
- Magazine pictures are shiny.
- It's good to reuse them, rather than throw them away.

Wrapping paper and greetings cards are fun because ...

- You can cover boxes, tubes, trays and cards.
- You can use them for découpage.
- You can use them to make gift tags.
- You can easily find pictures or patterns to suit the theme of your project.

Activities

Papier mâché bowls and trays (4+)

You can use just about any flexible container to make a papier mâché bowl, tray or box, as long as you smear it with Vaseline to prevent the papier mâché from sticking.

You will need

- Newspaper
- Plain white flour
- Water
- A bowl and whisk for making the paste
- Vaseline
- Flexible containers to act as moulds, such as plastic bowls and boxes, foil takeaway containers, foil cake and tart trays
- Ready mixed paint, PVA glue or varnish, brushes (for decorating)
- Other decorative items such as tissue paper, sequins, buttons, glass nuggets and stickers (optional)

What to do

Making the bowl / tray: using either the inside or the outside of the mould, smear the surface with a thin layer of Vaseline. Make a paste by mixing approximately 100g of flour with 250ml of water. Tear the newspaper into thin strips. Using plenty of flour mixture, paste the strips onto the mould. You can either apply the paste with a thick brush, or turn this into a 'messy play' activity by slapping on the paste with the fingers. Leave the papier mâché layer to dry and then repeat the process two or three times. If possible, pop it in an airing cupboard to speed up the drying process.

Decorating the bowl / tray: when the papier mâché is dry, paint it with brightly coloured ready mixed paints or acrylics. You can also stick on decorative items such as sequins and stickers. As an alternative to paint, paste on layers of tissue paper. Give the bowl a glossy finish with craft varnish or lightly diluted PVA glue (approximately one part water to five parts glue).

Use for

A pen tray: a papier mâché pen tray makes a good present. Use a flat aluminium foil tray as the mould for your papier mâché. When it's dry, trim the rough edges with scissors. Decorate the tray and finish off with varnish or PVA glue.

A pot pourri bowl: a home made papier mâché bowl filled with pot pourri makes a lovely present. Try to use strips of unprinted newspaper for the final layer of your bowl - save wrappings from the chip shop or use the unprinted edges of the newspaper page. When the papier mâché is dry, paste some layers of tissue paper onto the inside and outside of the bowl. Use pretty floral colours such as pink and pale green. Carefully stick some pressed flowers onto the outside of the bowl (*see Flower collage, page 114*). Fill the bowl with pot pourri.

Papier mâché balloons (4+)

A balloon makes a good mould for papier mâché. Once dry, you can release the balloon by popping it. The papier mâché balloon shape can then be used for various different projects.

You will need

- Newspaper
- Plain white flour
- Water
- A bowl and whisk for making the paste
- Vaseline
- Balloons
- Ready mixed paint, PVA glue or varnish, brushes (for decorating)
- Felt-tipped pens
- Other decorative items such as tissue paper, sequins and stickers (optional)

What to do

Blow up the balloon and keep it steady by resting it in the opening of a large saucepan. Smear the balloon with Vaseline and cover the entire surface with layers of papier mâché. Leave just a small opening at the tied end of the balloon. When the papier mâché is dry, burst the balloon and pull it out. Have fun decorating it (*see Papier mâché bowls and trays, page 96*).

Use for

Pigs: tape cardboard cylinders to a papier mâché balloon to make four legs and a snout. Cut out a pink card spiral to make the tail and card triangles for ears. Paint the pig a bright pink and stick on black card circles to make the eyes.

Mexican piñatas: a piñata is a hollow papier mâché shape filled with sweets. A traditional feature of Mexican festivities, the festival goers bash at the piñata with a stick until it breaks and releases a shower of goodies. Use a papier mâché balloon to make your own piñata. Decorate it with bright colours and fill with sweets. Sew wool from one side of the opening to the other to make a handle and hang it from a hand held stick or a hook in the ceiling. Let the children take turns at bashing it until it breaks and releases the sweets.

Masks: using a felt-tipped pen, mark out the shape of the mask on the balloon. Spread Vaseline over the mask shape and cover with several layers of papier mâché. Leave spaces for the eyes and mouth, moulding the edges of the holes to make smooth openings. When the papier mâché is dry, glue on a cardboard nose and ears. Paint the mask with acrylic or ready mixed paint and finish off with hair made from wool or shredded cellophane.

Maracas: use small round balloons and apply several layers of papier mâché to make a tough shell. When it's completely dry, fill the hollow balloon shape with lentils or dried peas. Tape over the opening with masking tape and attach a cardboard cylinder to make a handle. Decorate with colourful painted patterns and add a coat of craft varnish.

Papier mâché with wallpaper paste

Papier mâché can be made using wallpaper paste, as well as a flour and water mixture. Make sure you buy a variety that does not contain fungicide or other toxic additives.

Paper pulp (5+)

Paper pulp is another version of papier mâché. Because the paper is turned into a pulp rather than applied in strips, it is useful for modelling and moulding into relief shapes.

You will need

- Newspaper
- Water
- PVA glue
- Large mixing bowl
- Stiff card (for a background)
- Ready mixed or acrylic paints (for decorating)

What to do

To make the pulp, tear the newspaper into tiny pieces and moisten with a small amount of water. Mix in the PVA glue to make a thick, pulpy paste. Draw shapes on the stiff card and apply the pulp, moulding it with the fingers to make smooth surfaces, ridges and bumps. Put the pulp covered card in an airing cupboard to dry overnight. Once the pulp is dry, you can decorate it with ready mixed or acrylic paint. Finish off with craft varnish or a PVA glaze.

Use for

Picture frames: cut out a frame from stiff card, using a craft knife, metal ruler and wooden board (for adult use only – *see USING A CRAFT KNIFE box, page 90*). Cover the frame with paper pulp. Make a relief pattern by pressing the fingers into the pulp to create dents. When the pulp is dry, paint with acrylic paints and stick on sequins, beads or buttons. Finish off with a coat of PVA glue or craft varnish.

Monsters: paper pulp can be added to pictures of monsters to make beetling brows or lumpy, pock marked skin. If you intend to add pulp to a picture, always work on stiff card.

Animals: paper pulp is great for adding texture to animals. Give crocodiles, dinosaurs and toads a bumpy, warty skin with paper pulp. When the pulp is dry, paint over the surface. Add markings to your animal with techniques such as spraying and flicking paint (*see Spraying paint, page 28 and Dribbling and flicking paint, page 27*).

Drying paper pulp

Like papier mâché, paper pulp needs to be dried as quickly as possible, to avoid it smelling musty. Keep the layers thin and put the project in an airing cupboard to speed up the drying process.

Magazine montage (3+)

Magazines and comics offer a wealth of images to use for collage so magazine montage is a useful art activity to do in conjunction with a particular theme or topic.

You will need

- A selection of magazines and other publications such as household catalogues, seed catalogues, leaflets, brochures and comics
- Scissors
- PVA glue
- Card or sturdy paper (for a background)

What to do

Let older children leaf through the magazines and catalogues, selecting and cutting out pictures by themselves. Encourage them to create interesting shapes by tearing out the images, as well as cutting. Younger ones find it easier to choose images if they are given single pages to work from. Pick out pages that will interest the child and fit in with a particular theme. Choose a coloured background to set off the montage and encourage children to experiment with the arrangement of their collage pieces. Once they are happy with the composition of their picture, they can do the final sticking.

Use for

Funny people: go through magazines, cutting out heads, torsos, arms and legs. Put together different body parts to create funny people or Frankenstein's monsters. You may need to help the children to choose body parts that are roughly the same size – although a huge head and tiny legs or a big torso and tiny arms can add to the effect!

Crazy animals: this project uses a similar technique to 'Funny people' except that you use animal parts. Make up composite names based on the animals used in the collage – a girelephant could be a cross between a giraffe and an elephant; a camelbra could be a cross between a zebra and a camel.

Dinner time: cut out magazine pictures of food and stick them onto a large paper plate. Before sticking on the food, decorate the rim of the plate using different paint patterns (*see Brush effects, page 25*).

A flower garden: make a green and brown garden background using different techniques (*see Brush effects, page 25, Spraying paint, page 28, Wax rubbings, page 50, Bean bundle printing, page 110*). Cut out pictures from a seed catalogue and stick them on to the background to make a beautiful flower garden.

Traffic jam: cut out a wide strip of black paper. Use a flat ended brush to paint white stripes down the centre of the road (*see Brush effects / Rectangles, page 26*) or stick on strips of white paper. Find different vehicles in magazines, cut them out and stick them onto the road to make a traffic jam.

Tips for cutting

- It is easier to cut out images or shapes from smaller pieces of paper. When a child has chosen a picture, cut roughly around it, leaving a wide margin. The child can then complete the cutting out.
- Older children tend to cut quite quickly. Encourage them to slow down and cut carefully along the pencil lines.
- Provide plastic covered, blunt ended scissors for little ones.
- Check that scissors are safe but also make sure they cut well, otherwise the children will become frustrated.
- Provide left handed scissors for left handed children.
- Look out for scissors that cut wavy or zig-zag lines.

Magazine mosaic (6+)

Magazines encompass a huge range of different colours and shades. Make the most of this by cutting magazine pictures into small coloured squares for paper mosaics.

You will need

- Coloured pictures torn from magazines
- Scissors
- PVA glue
- Small containers for storing the mosaic squares
- Sturdy paper or thin card (as a background)
- Pencils

What to do

Go through the magazine pictures, finding different areas of colour. Cut the coloured areas into strips and then cut the strips into squares. Have a separate container for each colour and sort the squares into their correct container as you go. When you have enough squares, draw a simple design on paper or card. Cover part of the drawing with glue and stick on the mosaic pieces. Continue until the mosaic is completed.

Use for

Abstract mosaics: the simplest form of mosaic is an abstract design, where you simply arrange the squares to make a random shape. Challenge the children to produce a mosaic with shades of colour, working from light blue to dark blue and so on.

Roman pavements: study some pictures of ancient Roman mosaics and make mosaic pictures based on classical Roman designs.

Mosaic squares

Small mosaic squares can be quite fiddly to cut out and handle. Younger children can make mosaics using just a few larger squares. Help them to choose the colours they like and show them how to try different arrangements before sticking their squares onto the card background.

Mixed media with newspaper (all ages)

Newspaper can look surprisingly effective when combined with paints and other materials to produce what is known as a 'mixed media' artwork.

Black and White Rabbit by Hannah (7)

You will need

- Sheets of newspaper
- Scissors
- PVA glue
- Card (as a background)
- A variety of other art media such as paint, chalks, wax crayons, collage materials

What to do

Make a picture using a variety of different media. Show the children different ways of adding newspaper to their mixed media pictures.

Tearing: like tissue paper, newspaper tears easily and the torn edges are visually interesting. Tear into strips and shapes.

Crumpling: crumple the newspaper into loose balls and stick firmly to the background.

Words and pictures: cut individual words and pictures from a newspaper to add to a collage. Look out for headings and titles printed in large letters.

Painting: stippling, blobs and strokes of thick paint (*see Brush effects, page 25*) can all look effective on newspaper, as can spraying and flicking paint (*see Spraying paint, page 28 and Dribbling and flicking paint, page 27*). Choose bold primary colours to contrast with the more subtle black and white of the newspaper. Try tearing a shape from newspaper and then decorating it with paint, before adding it to the collage.

Mounting: newspaper makes an interesting mount for certain pictures. Glue a bold black and white drawing to a torn newspaper shape and mount on black or white card.

Use for

Cubist collage: Cubist painters such as Braques and Picasso were amongst the first artists to turn collage into an art form and they often used newspaper as part of their pictures. Try making your own mixed media Cubist pictures with newspaper print words, pieces of wallpaper and wood effect paper.

A note of caution

Before letting children loose on newspapers and magazines, check that they do not contain inappropriate stories and pictures. If in doubt, give the children carefully chosen single pages to work with.

Wrapping paper découpage (4+)

Découpage is a traditional craft activity used to decorate boxes, trays and other items. Wrapping paper offers a good source of motifs and it is easy to find a design or pattern to suit the theme of your project.

You will need

• Wrapping paper
• Scissors
• PVA glue
• A thick brush
• Items to decorate such as trays and boxes

What to do

Cut the wrapping paper into small shapes. Paste them onto the surface of the item with PVA glue. Build up layers of wrapping paper, overlapping the pieces and making sure that you finish with a layer of glue, which will dry to a clear finish.

Tip

Most craft shops and schools suppliers sell plain card and wooden items for decorating.
Look out for boxes, frames and ready cut card shapes to use as a base for découpage.

Use for

Trays, gift boxes and pencil pots: cover the lid of a shoe box with wrapping paper découpage to make a stationery or cuff link tray – a good present for the men in the family. Cover lidded boxes and cylinders to make gift boxes and pencil holders.

A greetings card: cover the front of a folded card with appropriate wrapping paper découpage. Choose flowers for Mother's Day cards, cartoon characters for children or seasonal motifs for Christmas, Diwali cards or Easter cards.

Picture frames: cut out a wide frame of stiff card and cover with découpage. Choose colours and patterns to suit the picture or photo you intend to frame.

Greetings cards motifs (all ages)

Save old greetings cards and use them as a source of motifs for sticking activities. The motifs can also be turned into attractive homemade cards or gift tags.

Gift tag

You will need

- Old greetings cards
- Scissors
- PVA glue
- Thin card in a variety of colours

What to do

Go through the cards, choosing pictures and motifs. Cut out the pictures for very young children and leave older ones to cut out their own. Set out the pictures on a card background, encouraging the children to experiment with the arrangement of their pieces. Once they have a composition they are happy with, they can stick on the pictures with PVA glue.

Use for

Gift tags: choose a single picture or motif. Cut it out and stick it to the centre of a small square or rectangle of card. Choose a card to complement the colours of the motif, or use a sturdy

handmade paper. Punch a hole in the corner of the card with a hole puncher, and thread ribbon through the hole to make a tie for the gift tag. Add small sequins or sticky stars.

Calendars: greetings card motifs make attractive calendars. Arrange and stick the pieces onto a stiff card background, add a small paper calendar and a ribbon loop so that the calendar can be hung on the wall.

Chapter 7

Beans and pasta, flowers and leaves

About beans and pasta

Dried beans and pulses make a surprisingly versatile resource. They come in all sorts of colours, sizes and shapes, ranging from tiny green mung beans and dark red aduki beans to large, flat butter beans and pretty pale green flageolets. They can be used in different ways; large beans, such as butter beans or split peas, can be stuck on individually, small pulses and grains, such as lentils or rice, can be sprinkled onto glue, like glitter.

Dry pasta can be used in different ways too. There are lots of shapes to explore, ranging from long thin spaghetti to large flat sheets of lasagne. Look out also for shapes such such as bows, shells, wheels, spirals and tubes. There's not such a variety of colours as beans and pulses but pasta is easy to paint and you can add a coat of craft varnish or a PVA glaze to bring out the colours.

Both beans and pasta can be fiddly to stick onto a background. Choose beans that are relatively easy to stick, such as flat-bottomed split peas rather than round chickpeas. An easier alternative is to press the items into a layer of Plasticine. A coat of craft varnish or PVA glue will help to hold the beans secure, as well as adding a glossy sheen.

Young children working with dried beans need to be supervised closely. Beans and pulses are quite easy to choke on and many are toxic prior to cooking. Red kidney beans are a particular culprit so avoid these. Aduki beans also have a rich red colour so use these instead.

About flowers

Pressed flowers (pressed in a flower press or between the pages of a heavy book) are lovely to use. You can also dry brightly coloured petals such as roses or chrysanthemums. Spread out the petals on a tray and leave the tray in the bottom of an airing cupboard until the petals are crisp. Pressing and drying are good ways of using up cut flowers that are getting a bit past it. Press the leaves and any flower heads that are still fresh, and harvest the loose petals for drying.

Beans and pasta, flowers and leaves

You can also try using dried flowers such as small chrysanthemum heads, statice and lavender (available from florists and craft shops). Stick the flowers onto collage backgrounds or use them to decorate crowns, boxes, wooden spoons and clay models. Dried herbs, old pot pourri and lavender flowers can also be saved for collage. Sprinkle them onto glue to add delicate colours, textures and scent to a picture.

About leaves

Leaves can be pressed too although autumn leaves can often be used without pressing, but they do need careful handling if they have become very dry. It is also possible to buy small packs of skeleton leaves from craft shops. These are beautiful, but quite expensive – save them for special projects and use them as the centrepiece of a collage or a mixed media picture.

Find as wide a variety of leaves as possible. Oak trees, silver birch, weeping willows, maples and horse chestnuts will provide a good range of shapes and sizes. Don't forget to collect leaves from plants too – dandelions, geraniums and ferns all have unusual and interesting shapes. Feathery grasses can also be added to a flower or leaf collage. Apart from collage, leaves can also be used to make charming prints and wax rubbings. Look out for leaves with interesting outline shapes and a raised pattern of veins. Always check both sides of the leaf. The veins on the underside of the leaf tend to be more raised, which makes for a clearer wax rubbing.

A note of caution

Before gathering leaves and flowers from woodlands, coastal areas and the countryside, check that you are not contravening any bye-laws. Many wild flowers are protected and should not be picked. If in doubt, stick to your own garden or use bought flowers.

Beans and pasta are fun because ...

- They offer lots of different colours and shapes
- They can be pressed into Plasticine to decorate boxes, plaques and other items

Use flowers in your artwork ...
- To remind you of summer days
- To add colour and scent
- To make a picture pretty

Use leaves in your artwork ...
- To make wax rubbings
- To make prints
- To add interesting shapes and textures

Activities

Bean and Plasticine collage (all ages)

Sticking beans onto a card background can be fiddly. Pressing them into a layer of Plasticine is much easier, enabling the children to focus on the design of their artwork.

You will need

- Plasticine
- A rolling pin
- Card (to make a background)
- PVA glue
- A variety of dried beans and pulses
- Craft varnish
- Thin ribbon
- Sticky tape

What to do

Roll the Plasticine into a layer, at least half a centimetre thick. Cut the card into whatever shape you need for a particular project (see Use for section below) and glue the layer of Plasticine to the card. Press the beans and pulses into the Plasticine to make a pattern. Younger ones can simply enjoy the process of choosing beans to press into the Plasticine. Older ones can create a pattern, using the different shapes and colours of the beans. When the collage is completed, check that all the beans are pressed in firmly and brush over with a PVA glaze (approximately one part water to five parts glue) or craft varnish (for adult use only). A coat of varnish will help to hold the beans secure and add a glossy finish.

Use for

Bean Plaques by Sarah (4) and Michael (10)

A wall plaque: cut out a card circle, rectangle, square or diamond and glue on a layer of Plasticine. Encourage older children to design a pattern of beans and pulses. Base the design around simple shapes such as a large star or concentric circles. When the plaque is finished, give it a coat of varnish and tape a loop of ribbon to the back. Hang the plaque on the wall or lean it against a sturdy plate stand.

Beans and pasta, flowers and leaves

Picture frames: use a craft knife and metal ruler to cut out a card frame (*see box on page 90*). Glue Plasticine to the frame and decorate with beans and pulses. Finish off with a coat of varnish.

Decorated boxes: for this project, you will need a small, sturdy box with a lid. You can either cover the whole lid with a layer of Plasticine, or cut out a card shape to stick onto the lid. As with the wall plaque, a simple design is best for showing off the different colours and shapes of the beans.

Tip
Most craft shops and schools suppliers sell plain card and wooden items for decorating. Look out for boxes, frames and ready cut card shapes to use as a base for bean and Plasticine collage.

Decorating clay (4+)

Beans and pulses make an attractive decoration for clay plaques, bowls and models.

You will need

- A variety of beans and pulses
- Clay
- PVA glue

What to do

Press beans and pulses into the wet surface of clay models, bowls and plaques. Check that the beans are pressed in far enough before leaving the clay to dry. Sometimes, clay shrinks during the drying process and the beans work loose. If this happens, secure them with a small blob of PVA glue. Finish off with a coat of craft varnish or PVA glaze.

Use for

Inside bowls or on the rims: make a shallow clay bowl and decorate the inside of the bowl with beans and pulses. Choose simple shapes such as concentric circles or lines radiating out from the centre of the bowl. Make a bowl with thick sides and press beans and pulses into the rim of the bowl.

Decorative clay plaques: make a clay plaque. Decorate it with rows of beans and pulses, interspersed with rows of markings.

An autumnal candle holder: this is a nice activity to do in conjunction with Harvest Festival. Roll a ball and make a candle holder using terracotta clay. Decorate the candle holder by pressing beans, pulses, small autumn leaves, acorns, beech nuts and twigs into the wet clay. Leave space to tie an orange ribbon round the middle of the candle holder and slot in a yellow, red or green candle.

Clay animals: small beans and pulses are useful for adding texture and markings to clay animals, particularly reptiles, insects and dinosaurs. Give frogs, toads and crocodiles a bumpy, warty skin with small green mung beans. Decorate the body of a spider with black kidney beans. Use split peas and black eye beans to add texture to dinosaurs.

Bean bundle printing (3+)

Make a bundle of beans with a square of cotton or muslin and use for printing textured backgrounds.

You will need

- A selection of beans and pulses, including large items such as chickpeas, and small items such as split lentils
- Squares of cotton or muslin
- Thread or thin string
- A paint pad (*see Simple printing, page 41*)
- A shallow container of paint
- A thick brush
- Sugar paper for the printing

Patchwork Landscape by Rachel (11)

What to do

Spread out a square of cotton and place a small pile of beans or pulses in the centre of the square. Using the thread, tie the cotton square into a bundle. Hold the bundle by the ends and cover it with paint, either by pressing it onto a paint pad, dipping it directly in the paint container or using a paint brush. Press the painty bean bundle onto sugar paper to make prints. Compare the prints made by large grains such as chickpeas with small grains such as rice.

Use for

Landscapes: use bean bundles and green and brown paint to print textured fields and hills. Single prints can also be used to represent bushes and the foliage of trees.

Animals: use bean bundles to print the bodies of animals and add details with a felt-tipped pen or cut-out card shapes.

Decorative borders: use bean bundles to print around the borders of mounting paper, frames and the pages of handmade books.

Pasta beads (3+)

Pasta tubes can be painted and threaded onto ribbon or cord to make pretty necklaces.

Beads made from painted penne pasta

You will need

- Pasta tubes, such as penne and macaroni
- A knitting needle and Plasticine
- Ready mixed or acrylic paint
- Thick and thin brushes
- Craft varnish (for adult use only) or PVA glue
- Glitter glue pens

What to do

Thread the pasta tubes on to knitting needles and rest the needle between two lumps of Plasticine. Paint the pasta with bright colours and leave it to dry. Nimble fingered older children can also use a thin brush to paint spots, stripes or zig-zags onto the larger tubes. Give the pasta beads a coat of craft varnish or PVA glue to bring out the colours of the paint. When the glaze is completely dry, add some small blobs of glitter glue.

Use for

Necklaces and bracelets: thread the pasta onto a ribbon and tie a knot to make a pasta necklace. Use short cut macaroni and thread onto thin elastic to make bracelets. Try interspersing the pasta with other home-made beads (*see HANDMADE BEADS box on page 112 for suggestions*).

Mobiles: thread a large round bead onto a length of ribbon or cord and tie a knot in the end to hold it secure. Thread decorated pasta tubes onto the ribbon, interspersing the tubes with more round beads (these can either be bought or hand made - *see HANDMADE BEADS box below for ideas*). Cover a wire coat hanger by winding it round with lengths of ribbon. Dangle lots of pasta and bead threaded ribbons from the coat hanger to make a mobile.

Handmade beads

A painted pasta necklace or mobile can be made more interesting by interspersing the pasta with handmade beads. For some more ideas on making your own beads, see:

- Paper beads (*page 77*)
- Clay beads (*page 160*)
- Marbled fimo beads (*page 78*)

Spaghetti block printing (7+)

Long, thin strands of spaghetti make interesting prints. Glue the spaghetti onto a wooden printing block to make it easier for the children to handle.

You will need

- Spaghetti
- Hand-sized wooden blocks (*see Card printing blocks, page 65*)
- PVA glue
- Ready mixed paint
- A medium-sized brush

What to do

Break the spaghetti into short lengths so that it will fit onto the wooden printing block. Spread a thick layer of PVA glue over the surface of the block and stick on the spaghetti.

Try out lots of different patterns:

Stripes: stick lengths of spaghetti side by side so that the lengths are touching. Make a pattern by printing the block horizontally, then vertically, then horizontally and so on.

Criss-crosses: stick lengths of spaghetti side by side with spaces in between each length. Try making a criss-cross pattern by printing horizontal lines on top of vertical lines.

Line prints: snap the spaghetti into short lengths and stick a row of horizontal pieces next to a row of vertical pieces.

Short and tall: stick on a series of spaghetti lengths, ranging from short to tall.

Beans and pasta, flowers and leaves

Curves: stick on a series of spaghetti lengths ranging from short to tall to short, to create a curved shape.

Abstract line patterns: stick different lengths of spaghetti randomly on the block to make an abstract pattern.

Leaf veins: stick short pieces of spaghetti onto a rectangular wood block to make a leaf vein pattern. Try printing onto a leaf shape cut from green paper.

Tip

Although the spaghetti is easy to snap into different lengths, it can be difficult to handle. With younger or less nimble fingered children, stick to making printing blocks with an abstract arrangement of lines. Be ready to help with making more complicated designs, such as leaf veins. To get a clear print from the delicate lines of spaghetti, do a run through on newspaper to blot up the excess paint. A spaghetti block can only be used a certain number of times before the spaghetti becomes soggy.

Use for

Decorative borders: spaghetti prints are good for decorating the borders of mounting paper, frames and the pages of home-made books.

Wrapping paper: print patterns of lines directly onto tissue paper. For a Christmassy touch, mix the paint with PVA glue and sprinkle glitter onto the prints.

Leaves: cut out lots of leaves from thin green card, checking that the leaves are the right size for the leaf vein printing block. For autumn trees, use colours such as orange, yellow, brown and red. Choose a paint that will show up on the leaves and print each leaf with a pattern of veins. Make a tree trunk from wax bark rubbings (*see page 50*) and stick on the leaves.

Pasta plaques

Using lots of PVA glue, stick pasta shapes to a square of stiff cardboard. Choose interesting shapes such as bows, tubes or spirals. When the glue is dry, spray the pasta with gold or silver paint. Tape a loop of ribbon to the back of the card and hang the pasta plaque on the wall.

Bean and pasta collage – some more ideas

Pasta bows: use farfalle bows to make bow ties and decorate collage clothes and hair.

Penne fences and walls: stick on rows of penne or rigatoni pasta to make picket fences and the walls of forts and castles. Paint the pasta brown or grey.

Split pea jewels: use split green and yellow peas to make the jewels on portraits of Tudor kings and queens.

Harvest Festival pictures: sprinkle small items such as lentils, rice, mustard and sesame seeds onto a landscape background. If the seeds are a bit loose, drip more PVA on top of the seeds. The glue will dry clear and hold the seeds secure.

Pasta seashells: paint pasta shells in white, grey and pale pink. Glaze the pasta with craft varnish or PVA and stick them onto a sandy background to make a seaside picture. If the shells are difficult to stick, press them into a small lump of yellow Plasticine.

Pasta snails: use the largest pasta shells you can find for this project. Paint the shell with dabs of grey and brown. Roll a small lump of Plasticine or clay into a sausage and stick it underneath the shell to make the snail's body.

Butter bean ladybirds: paint a butter bean bright red. When the paint is dry, stick on small dots of black card cut with a hole puncher. Glaze the ladybird with craft varnish or PVA glue.

Flower collage (3+)

Flowers make a beautiful resource for collage. There are three main ways of using them – fresh, dried or pressed.

You will need

- Fresh flower petals such as rose petals
- Fresh flower heads
- Dried flower heads
- Lavender flowers
- Pot pourri
- A flower press or several heavy books
- Card in brilliant white, plus a range of pastel colours
- PVA glue

What to do

Fresh flower collage: this makes a delightful sticking activity for very young children. If possible, let them gather their own flower petals. The petals need to be quite robust and brightly coloured – rose petals are ideal. Sort the petals into different containers according to colour. Work on brilliant white card as this will show off the petals to their best advantage. Put a dab of PVA glue on the card and stick a petal on top. Encourage the children to choose different coloured petals and enjoy their scent. The nature and appearance of the collage will alter from day to day as the petals dry out. Encourage the children to observe their changing artwork. Which do they prefer – the fresh petal collage or the dried petal collage?

Dried flower collage: use ready-dried flower heads, lavender flowers and pot pourri to make a collage picture. Work on a pastel coloured background such as pale pink, pale green or cream. Spread glue across the paper and sprinkle on lavender and pot pourri.

Stick on flower heads individually and add large seeds and spices such as pumpkin seeds, cloves and star anise.

Pressed flower collage: gather fresh flowers to press. Choose flowers with flat heads such as daisies, buttercups, poppies, primulas and pansies. The flowers need to be completely dry before pressing. Thin papery flowers such as poppies will usually press within a week or so, while flowers with thicker heads can take several weeks. The flowers should not be used until they are bone dry, otherwise they may go mouldy. If you do not have a flower press, lay the flowers carefully between sheets of blotting paper or paper towels and slip in between the pages of a telephone directory. Pile heavy books on top and leave the flowers for at least a week. You can check on their progress from time to time, as long as the flowers are not disturbed. Once they are completely dry, they can be glued onto a card background, using small dabs of PVA glue.

Use for

A vase of flowers: use painted patterns to make a pretty vase (*see Brush effects, page 25*) or cut out a vase from decorative paper such as marbled paper (*see Marbling, page 39*). Stick the vase onto a large card background and 'fill' it with flowers. Use a combination of dried flower heads, lavender, pot pourri and large pressed flowers and leaves.

A collage flower garden: make a garden background using green and brown wax rubbing patterns (*see Wax rubbings, page 50*), sponge painting and textured paper shapes (*see Textured paper collage, page 73*). Stick pressed leaves and dried flower heads to the background to turn it into a beautiful flower garden.

Pressed flower gift tags: choose small, pretty flower heads such as forget-me-nots, primulas and buttercups. Carefully glue the flowers to a circle of coloured card. Punch a hole with a hole puncher and thread with thin ribbon into a gift tag.

Pressed flower bookmarks: decorate a thin rectangle of card with pressed flowers. Punch a hole in one end of the card and thread through a ribbon or a silk tassel. Carefully stick a piece of clear sticky backed plastic over the flowers to protect them. As you lay the plastic over the flowers, smooth it with a folded paper towel to press out any wrinkles.

More ways to use dried flowers

Apart from collage, dried flowers can be used to decorate a variety of different items. Unless otherwise stated, the specialist items for the following projects can be purchased from most florist's shops.

Dried flower arrangement: for this activity, you will need dried flowers with long stems such as lavender and statice. You will also need some florist's foam and a pretty container or basket. Simply place the florist's foam into the container and push in the stems of the flowers. Even the youngest children can help with the arrangement to make a lovely Mother's Day or birthday gift.

Dried flower pomander: spread PVA glue over a ball of florist's foam or a polystyrene sphere (available from schools suppliers and craft shops). Stick dried flower heads

over the ball so that the surface is completely covered. Once the glue is dry, stick two lengths of ribbon crossways around the ball. Glue on a bow and a loop of ribbon so that the pomander can be hung on the wall.

Decorated plant pots: dried flower heads make a pretty decoration for terracotta flower pots. Stick the flower heads around the rim of the flower pot with dabs of PVA glue. As the decoration is not waterproof, use the pot as a holder for a ready-potted plant.

Decorated wood: dried flower heads are useful for decorating various card and wooden items such as frames, napkin rings, boxes and wooden spoons (*see Painting wooden spoons, page 151*).

Buying pressed flowers

Many craft shops now sell small packs of pressed flower heads. They can be quite expensive, but they are useful if you don't have time to press your own. The packs also tend to contain flowers of a similar shape and size.

Pressed leaf collage (3+)

Most leaves press well and they offer a wide range of different colours and shapes to use in collage.

You will need

- Leaves
- A flower press or several heavy books
- Card in a range of colours (for a background)
- PVA glue

What to do

Gather as wide a variety of leaves as possible, looking out for different shapes and colours. Press the leaves in a flower press or heavy book (*see Flower collage / Pressed flower collage, page 115*). Dry autumn leaves are particularly easy to press, whereas fresh spring leaves will take longer as they are still full of sap. Spring leaves may not hold their colour as well as autumn leaves. Once the leaves are bone dry, choose a card background to set them off. Brilliant white makes a good foil for richly coloured autumn leaves. For more delicate green leaves, choose a pastel background such as beige, cream, pale pink or pale green. You can also experiment with different background papers, such as a plain textured wallpaper or unbleached handmade paper. Once you have chosen the background, stick the leaves to the card with small dabs of PVA glue.

Beans and pasta, flowers and leaves

· ·

Use for

Free collage: leaf collage makes a good sticking activity for little children and the different shapes and colours result in an attractive picture, even when stuck randomly onto a background.

Pressed leaf window decal: an intricately shaped autumn leaf makes an effective window decal. Simply slip the leaves into a clear plastic folder and tape the folder to a window pane. Choose leaves with glowing autumn colours and beautiful shapes, such as acers (Japanese maples).

Creatures: use the shapes of the leaves to inspire different animal collages. Make a fish's scales by overlapping leaves from a silver birch tree. Add felt-tipped pen legs to a small, round leaf to make insects or stick the leaves in a line to make the body of a caterpillar. Use maple leaves to make the wings of birds. Turn spiky pressed dandelion leaves into dragons.

Decorated leaves (7+): press some large, sturdy leaves. Use a thin brush and acrylic paints to make simple patterns on the surface of the leaves. Spread PVA glue across a leaf and sprinkle on glitter. For a more natural look, decorate the leaves with tiny seeds such as sesame and mustard.

Trees: make a tree trunk with sponge painting or brown wax bark rubbings (*see page 50*). Stick pressed leaves to the branches of the tree. Add some cut-out leaf prints and wax leaf rubbings (*see below*).

Christmas leaf decoration: choose sturdy pressed leaves with interesting shapes or use evergreen leaves such as ivy or holly (these leaves don't need pressing). Brush some water-based gold paint across the leaves. When the paint is dry, add a few dabs of PVA glue and sprinkle on some gold glitter. Glue the leaves to a wide Christmassy ribbon, interspersing each leaf with a small gold gift bow. Glue the end of the ribbon around a wooden curtain ring and hang up the decoration.

Leaf printing (4+)

Choose leaves with a strong pattern of veins for making prints. If you can find leaves that also have a long stalk, the children can use the stalk as a handle. This makes the leaf easier to manipulate during the printing process.

You will need

- Lots of different shaped leaves with clear patterns of veins
- Ready mixed paint
- Paint brush
- Sugar paper to print onto

· ·

What to do

Before introducing the activity to the children, experiment with each leaf type to make sure it gives a good print. Paint one side of the leaf with ready mixed paint and press down on the paper to make a print. If the leaf is not very flat, place a sheet of thin paper on top and press down gently to make sure that all parts of the leaf leave a print.

Use for

Wrapping paper and gift tags: make leaf prints on thin coloured paper or tissue paper and use as wrapping paper. You can also print directly onto the wrapped present, as long as the surface is flat. Use the same leaf to print a matching gift tag.

Seasonal trees: cut out different coloured leaf prints to make a 'seasonal trees' collage. Use a fresh, pale green for spring leaves. Use a strong, bright green for summer leaves. For autumn leaves, use red, orange, yellow and brown. Sponge paint four tree trunks and stick the printed leaves onto three of the trees to represent the three seasons. Leave the fourth tree bare to represent winter. You can also add pink tissue paper blossom to the spring tree (*see Tissue paper flowers, page 84*), collage apples or cherries to the summer tree and tufts of cotton wool 'snow' to the winter tree.

Leaf prints and rubbings

Use the same leaf to make a wax rubbing and a print. Which effect do the children prefer? Can they see that the outline shape and pattern of veins is the same on both the print and the rubbing? Remember to take the rubbing before you cover the leaf with paint to make a print.

Nature weaving (3+)

This is a lovely way of displaying your 'finds' from a walk. It also gives you a good excuse to get out into the woods or the park to gather items for your 'nature weaving'.

You will need

- A large sheet of stiff card
- Ready mixed paint and sponges
- Scissors
- 'Rustic' looking string such as raffia, twine or thick wool
- Sticky tape
- Long, thin 'nature' items for weaving, such as feathers, grasses, ears of wheat, long thin leaves, thin bendy twigs, strands of sheep's wool, flowers with long stems

What to do

Once you have a good collection of suitable nature items, you will need to make your weaving frame.

Beans and pasta, flowers and leaves

Sponge paint the card, using a natural colour to provide a good foil for the items.

Cut notches along the top and the bottom edges of the card, approximately 1 to 2 centimetres apart.

Tape the end of a length of string to the back of the card.

Wind the string up and down the card, using the notches to hold it secure.

Tape the other end to the back of the card.

Carefully weave the items in and out of the strings.

If any item looks as though it might slip, secure it with small blobs of PVA glue.

Tape a loop of ribbon to the back of the card so that the nature weaving can be hung on the wall.

> **Tip**
> *Look out for appropriate textured papers to use as a background for the weaving, and glue the paper onto the card. Try corrugated paper, a plain textured wallpaper or unbleached handmade paper.*

Chapter 8

Fabric and buttons, wool and string

About fabric and buttons

Fabric offers a never-ending range of colours, textures and patterns. Start a fabric scrap box and look out for interesting off-cuts in craft and haberdashery shops. You can also cut up old clothes and add the pieces to your collection. Fabric ranges from delicate silk and chiffon to robust and sturdy tweed (the fabric versions of tissue paper and stiff handmade card!). Aim to have lots of colours, patterns and textures, including cotton, net, satin, knitted fabrics, brocade, chiffon, linen and fake fur.

Many fabrics can be quite difficult to cut so give younger children ready cut pieces and provide older children with sharp scissors (carefully supervised, of course). Many fabrics also tend to fray at the edges. If children find this frustrating, show them how the fraying can add texture and interest to their fabric artwork (*see Fabric collage / Frayed edges, page 122*). If you want a non-fraying fabric, go for felt. With its bright, even colours and easy-to-cut texture it makes a good choice when you want bold shapes, strong colours and a material that will stand up to lots of handling. Even younger children can cut out felt for themselves.

Fabric collage needs a sturdy card background, particularly weightier fabrics such as tweed or felt. You can stick the fabric with ordinary PVA glue, although you may find that the glue shows through thinner fabrics such as silk. As with tissue paper, use tiny dabs of glue.

You can also paint or dye certain fabrics to create your own colours and patterns. If you want to decorate an item of clothing, you will need to use special fabric paints. These can be purchased from art and craft shops or schools suppliers, and they will stand up to being washed and worn. If you simply want to create patterned fabrics for a collage or craft activity, you can get away with ready mixed or acrylic paint. Always check that the fabric you intend to use is suitable for painting or dying.

Use buttons to add detail to a fabric collage. They are easy to stick onto a card background, as long as you choose the type with flat bases. Difficult shapes can be sewn onto fabric or pressed into Plasticine, before being stuck onto a background.

Fabric and buttons, wool and string

Children love rifling through a button box and choosing their favourites for collage and other artwork. Fill your box with a variety salvaged from old clothes. You can also buy single buttons from a haberdashery shop, which is useful if you need a special shape, size or colour for a particular project.

About wool and string

Wool also comes in a huge range of different colours, textures and thicknesses. Save the left-over wool from knitting, or look out for single balls in the sale basket of the haberdashery or craft shop. Thick, textured wools are the best for collage and weaving as they are easy to stick and create an attractive rough texture.

Raw wool can also be used for collage and weaving. If you live near sheep farming country, you may be able to gather strands of wool from hedges or fences. Wash the wool in detergent and dry it before the children handle it. Some craft shops also sell bags of raw wool intended for hand spinning and knitting.

Like wool, string comes in different thicknesses. Save odd scraps or look out for cheap balls in DIY and hardware shops. Although it is very attractive arranged in spirals, whirls and wiggly lines on a card background, string can be quite difficult for children to handle. Make it more manageable by turning it into a printing block or tube (*see String print blocks, page 129 and Printing with string tubes, page 130*). It can also be covered with chalk or paint and used to make some interesting rainbow patterns (*see Powdered chalk / Twanging string, page 58 and Folded paper string prints, page 130*).

There are many other threads and 'stringy things' that can be used in collage. Save bits of ribbon, lace, cord, embroidery silk and raffia for collage and weaving. For more 'stringy things' ideas, see the box on page 132.

Fabric and wool are fun because ...

- They add colour, texture and pattern to a collage.
- They can be used for weaving and threading.
- They can be decorated with special fabric paints, sequins, beads and other pretty bits and pieces.

Buttons are fun because ...

- They are easy to stick
- They come in all shapes and sizes
- They are great for decorating collage people

String is fun because ...

- It makes great prints
- You can turn it into spirals, whirls and wiggly lines
- You can use it to make weaving frames

Activities

Fabric collage (all ages)

Use the colours, textures and patterns of fabric to create some interesting collage pictures.

You will need

- Scraps of fabric
- Sharp scissors (for supervised use by older children only)
- A sturdy card background
- PVA glue
- Chalk

What to do

Cut up the fabric into small pieces for younger children. Provide older ones with chalk so that they can draw shapes on the fabric before cutting. Encourage the children to explore the composition of their picture, before sticking down the pieces. Introduce the following techniques:

Fabric backgrounds: make a fabric background by sticking two or three strips or a single large piece onto stiff card. Choose plain fabrics for the background and check that the colours provide a good foil for the fabric details.

Frayed edges: if you are using a fabric that frays, pull out some of the fibres to increase the frayed edge. Stick down the frayed fibres or leave them hanging loose.

Fringes: cut the edge of a piece of fabric into fringes. Stick the fabric onto the card so that the fringe is left hanging loose.

Knots: cut thin fabric into strips and tie the strips into knots before sticking them onto the card.

Plaits: plait three thin strips of fabric together and stick onto the card.

Crumples: crumple up a piece of thin fabric and stick it onto the card in the form of a clump rather than a flat shape.

Use for

Abstract collage: show off the different colours, textures and patterns of the fabric with an abstract collage. Cut the fabric into strips and random shapes. Arrange them on the background to make an interesting composition.

Lots of textures: see how many contrasting textures you can include in an abstract fabric collage: rough tweed, shiny satin, smooth silk, fluffy fake fur fabric, soft cotton wool.

Fabric and buttons, wool and string

Clothes: paint a person on a large piece of paper and dress him or her with fabric collage clothes. Add real buttons, ribbons and laces.

Coloured areas: gather together scraps of fabric in the same colour. Cut the fabric into small pieces and use to make an area of textured colour – brown scraps for a tree trunk, green scraps for a field, blue and green scraps for the sea.

Fabric weaving (5+)

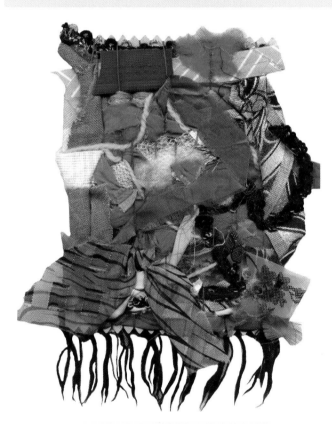

Fabric Weaving by Hannah (10)

Fabric weaving is a simple way of displaying samples from your fabric collection. It is most effective if you use fabrics from a similar colour group, for example reds, pinks, lilacs and purples.

You will need

- Stiff card
- Scissors
- String
- Tape
- Strips of fabric cut into different widths and lengths

What to do

Make the weaving card by cutting notches along the top and bottom edges of the card, approximately 1cm apart. Tape the end of a length of string to the back of the card.

Wind the string up and down the card, using the notches to hold the string secure. Tape the other end of the string to the back of the card.

Carefully weave strips of fabric in and out of the strings. Aim to fill the card so that you cannot see the strings or the card. The weaving does not have to be very regular. If you come to the end of a fabric strip in the middle of the card, just start a new strip. Tuck in small strips of fabric to fill any gaps.

> **Tip**
> *The finished weaving will be quite heavy. Rest it against a sturdy plate holder and display it on a shelf or mantelpiece.*

There are lots of decorative little items that can be added to fabric artwork. Check out the haberdashery or craft shop for the following:

- Lace • Brocade • Tassels • Appliqués
- Bows • Sequins • Beads • Decorative buttons

Using buttons (4+)

There are two main ways of using buttons in art and craft – sticking them onto a background and sewing them onto fabric pieces.

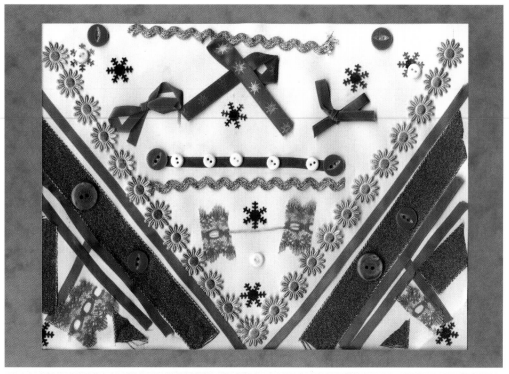

Buttons and Bows by Eleanor (8)

You will need

- Buttons in a variety of colours and sizes
- Medium weight fabric such as sturdy cotton, felt or linen
- Needle and thread
- PVA glue
- A stiff card background

What to do

Buttons with flat bases are easy to stick onto a card background. Use them to decorate paintings, collage and other pictures.

Fabric and buttons, wool and string

Sew buttons onto fabric and stick the fabric onto a card background. This technique enables you to use buttons with shapes that are not suitable for sticking.

> **Tip**
> *As a quick alternative to sewing difficult shapes onto fabric, try pressing the button into a lump of Plasticine. Smooth out the base of the Plasticine before sticking it onto a stiff card background.*

Use for

Decorating frames and boxes: cut fabric into the right shape to cover a box lid or a frame cut from stiff card. Sew buttons onto the fabric and then stick the fabric onto the frame or the box. Choose different sized buttons and go for colours that complement each other. Choose a fabric colour to set off the colour of the buttons.

Decorating people pictures: add an authentic touch to paintings or collage pictures of people by sticking on flat based buttons.

A button wall plaque: cut out a small square or circle of stiff card. Arrange the buttons in a pattern and stick them onto the card with PVA glue. Tape a loop of ribbon to the back of the card and hang your button plaque on the wall.

Felt storyboard figures (4+)

Storyboard figures are cut-out character shapes that can be attached to a board with magnetic tape or Velcro hooks. Children love moving the figures about the board and using them to tell stories. The activity is even more fun if you make your own figures from bits of coloured felt.

You will need

- Stiff card
- Pencils
- Scissors
- Felt in lots of different colours
- Thin felt-tipped pens
- PVA glue
- Velcro hooks or magnetic tape
- A large, felt covered board or a magnetic white board

What to do

Choose characters that can be used for telling stories:

- Characters from a picture book • Fairy-tale characters • Nursery rhyme characters
- Family members • Friends • Favourite animals • Space aliens • Monsters
- Computer game characters • Characters from a TV programme • Characters from a film

Cut out shapes for your figures from card. Cut the felt into small pieces and stick them onto the card to decorate the figures. Make sure that no card is showing. To turn the figures into storyboard characters, glue a square of Velcro hooks to the back of the figure so that it can be 'stuck' to a large felt covered board. Alternatively, stick on strips of magnetic tape and use the figures on a magnetic white board. Before using the figures, check that everything is firmly stuck. If the children play with the figures regularly, you may need to re-stick the pieces of felt from time to time.

Sock puppets (3+)

Old socks make a quick and easy base for a puppet - and children love playing with a puppet character that they have created for themselves.

You will need

- Old socks
- Bits of coloured felt
- Scissors
- PVA glue
- Needle and cotton
- Buttons, beads and other decorative bits and pieces

What to do

Check that the sock fits comfortably over the child's hand. Sew buttons onto the toe of the sock to make eyes. Cut out lots of felt circles, strips and other shapes and glue or sew them onto the sock to make the puppet's features. Add other details such as small woollen pompoms, bows, strands of wool to make hair and pieces of fur fabric. Double check that everything is securely attached, before letting the children play with their sock puppets.

> **Tip**
> *You can also use old mittens to make puppets.*

Decorating T-shirts (3+)

Use specialist fabric paints to decorate a T-shirt. As long as you follow the instructions on the pack, your garment should stand up to being worn and washed.

You will need

- Large sheets of paper and felt-tipped pens (for planning a design)
- Specialist fabric paints (available from art and craft shops and schools suppliers)
- A plain cotton T-shirt
- Brushes
- Decorative items such as small bows, buttons, beads, sequins and appliqués (optional)

Fabric and buttons, wool and string

What to do

Look out for T-shirts in budget shops and charity shops. Some schools suppliers also sell plain T-shirts for decorating. Check the instructions on the pack of fabric paint to ensure that the fabric is suitable for painting. Draw around the T-shirt on a large piece of paper and use felt-tipped pens to design a pattern, sticking to simple shapes such as hearts, flowers, football team emblems and slogans. Make a design for the back as well as the front, and add small patterns around the neckline, sleeves and bottom. Copy the design onto the T-shirt with fabric paint, following the instructions on the back of the pack. Some paints recommend that you iron the finished item before washing.

Fabric paints can be used in the same way as ordinary paint – try the following techniques:

Brush effects (*page 25*): try dots, fans, squares and stippling. Decorate the front and back of the shirt with rows of brush effects. Sew on rows of buttons, bows, appliqués and other small items between the print patterns.

Dribbling and flicking paint (*page 27*): to make an abstract design, flick different coloured paints across the front and back of the shirt. Add random splodges, splashes and dribbles of paint.

Spraying paint (*page 28*): spray paint across the T-shirt to make a misty background for appliqués or large painted motifs.

Simple printing (*page 41*): use sponge shapes, half potatoes and cotton reels to print patterns on the T-shirt.

Body part prints (*page 43*): hand prints make a fun decoration and even the youngest children can join in.

Card block prints (*page 65*): cut card into simple shapes such as geometric shapes, flowers or hearts. This technique is useful for creating strong, clear outlines.

String block prints (*page 129*): string spirals printed around the neckline and the hem of the shirt look particularly effective. Sew buttons or small pieces of ribbon in between the prints.

Tip
Many schools suppliers sell fabric pens and crayons, as well as fabric paints. Use them for fine details and writing slogans.

Decorating fabric items

There are many other fabric items that can be decorated – try plain cotton bags and pencil cases, fabric hats, trousers and handkerchiefs. Glue flat based rhinestones to bags and trousers, and sew on decorative buttons and appliqués. Paint bold, colourful designs around the brim of a hat and down the legs of trousers.

Tie-dying (3+)

Tie-dying is a simple way of decorating fabric and creates the most striking results. It works best with natural fibres such as cotton or silk. Always study the instructions on the pack of dye to check which fabrics are recommended for dying.

You will need

- Cold water fabric dye
- Fabric, preferably made from natural fibres such as cotton or silk
- String

What to do

Make up the fabric dye according to the instructions. Tie the corners of the fabric in knots and tie string around parts of the fabric to make an untidy bundle. Following the instructions, dye the bundle of fabric. When it is dry, undo the knots and spread out the fabric to reveal the beautiful tie-dye patterns. Follow the instructions for washing the fabric and ironing out the creases.

Tip
Experiment with colour combinations. Dye the bundle of fabric in one colour. When it has dried, re-tie the bundle and dye it again using a different colour. Always use the lighter colour first, for example yellow followed by blue or pink followed by green.

A note of caution

Although fabric dye shouldn't be toxic, it is not designed for use by children. Supervise this activity very carefully, particularly with younger children.

Use for

T-shirts: tie-dye is an effective way of decorating plain cotton T-shirts and other items of clothing.

Silk scarves: for a special gift, tie-dye a square of silk to make a scarf.

Tie-dye collage: tie-dye small pieces of fabric and use them as part of a fabric collage picture.

String print blocks (4+)

String is great for printing because it can be twisted and curved into spirals, whirls and other shapes and patterns. Stick the string onto wooden blocks to make it easier to handle.

You will need

- String
- Wooden printing blocks (*see Card printing blocks, page 65*)
- PVA glue
- Paint and brush
- Sugar paper for printing

What to do

Spread glue across the surface of the wood block and stick on the string. When the glue is dry, paint the string block and use to make prints. Try different patterns such as tight spirals, loose spirals, letters (use alongside matchstick printing block letters with straight lines, such as H and T), wiggly lines or scribbles.

Use for

Borders and frames: string print spirals make a good decoration for the borders of mounting paper, the pages of homemade books and picture frames.

T-shirts and trousers: use a spiral string block and fabric paints to decorate clothing (*see Decorating T-shirts, page 126*).

Snails: use a loose spiral print to decorate a cut-out card snail shell.

Pig's tails: use a loose spiral printing block and pink paint to print a pig's curly tail.

Seahorses: use a loose spiral printing block to print a seahorse's curly tail.

Fish: use a tight spiral printing block with pale blue, green and silver paint to print the scales of a fish.

Hair: use tight spirals to print curly hair and beards onto paintings of faces.

Decorative paper and wrapping paper: use wiggly line prints and scribbles to decorate mounting paper or wrapping paper.

Personalised cards: use string block letters to print personalised greetings cards. Print the recipient's initials in the centre of the card and surround them with a decorative border.

'Signatures': use string block initials to print a special 'signature' on a painting.

Printing with string tubes (4+)

A cardboard tube wrapped around with string makes a simple but effective printing object.

You will need

- Sturdy cardboard cylinders
- String
- PVA glue
- Ready mixed, powder or acrylic paint
- Paint brushes
- White cartridge paper and different coloured sugar papers (for printing)

What to do

Spread a thin layer of glue on the surface of the tube and wrap string around it. When the glue is dry, brush different coloured paint onto the string. Show the children how to hold the tube at either end and roll it across the paper to leave rainbow coloured string tracks.

Use for

Decorative paper: use rainbow string prints to decorate mounting paper or wrapping paper.

Covering boxes: use the paper to cover boxes and other items (*see Cylinder collage, page 71, Collage with boxes, page 70, Towers and totem poles, page 72*).

Folded paper string prints (3+)

Pulling painty string through a sheet of folded paper is perhaps the simplest way of creating a string print. The results are surprisingly effective.

You will need

- String
- Ready mixed paint
- Brushes
- White cartridge paper
- Newspaper

What to do

You will need at least two people to do this activity. Fold the cartridge paper in half. Place a length of string on the newspaper and brush it with dabs of different coloured paints. Make sure the string is well covered with paint. Leave the two ends paint free so that you can handle the string without getting your fingers covered with paint. Lay the string in between the folded paper with one end sticking out. Cover the folded paper with

a couple of sheets of newspaper and get one person to press down on the newspaper while the other person pulls out the string. Open out the paper to reveal the pattern.

Use for

Birds, butterflies and flowers: fold over a sheet of coloured paper and draw half a bird, butterfly or flower against the fold. Cut out the drawing and open it up to reveal the symmetrical shape of your butterfly, bird or flower. Refold the shape, place the painty string inside and drag it out to create a rainbow pattern.

Collage with 'stringy things' (4+)

Wool, ribbon, string and other threads make attractive and unusual collages.

Stringy Things Wall Hanging by Michael (10)

You will need

- A collection of 'threads' such as wool, string and embroidery silks plus ribbons, laces and cords (*see MORE 'STRINGY THINGS' box on page 132 for further suggestions*)
- Scissors
- PVA glue
- A sturdy card background
- Felt pens, pencils and paints (optional)

What to do

Choose materials to suit the age group of the children. Little ones cope better with wider items such as ribbon, sturdy lace and thick wool. Challenge older ones to work with thinner threads such as string and embroidery silks.

Cut the background card into an interesting shape such as a circle or a simple star. Cut the string, wool, threads and ribbons into different lengths. Spread a stripe of PVA glue across the card background and stick on a length of ribbon or string. Stick on some of the pieces so that they overlap each other and the edges of the shape. Challenge older ones to arrange the string and thread in wiggly lines and curves.

> **Tip**
> *It is much easier to spread the glue on the paper and then place the string and wool on top of the glue. However, older ones can try applying the glue directly onto wider items such as ribbons and lace.*

Use for

Exploring 'line' with mixed media: combine the threads with paint, pencil and felt pen lines as part of a project on 'line' in art.

Wall hanging: stick several circular 'stringy thing' collages to a wide strip of ribbon and hang on the wall.

More 'stringy things'

Apart from string, ribbon and wool, try the following long, thin items for collage and weaving:

• metallic thread • cotton • button thread • embroidery silk • silk cord
• lace • velvet ribbon • sequin strips • shoe laces • darning wool
• raffia • garden twine • gift ribbon • feathery grasses • stalks of straw

Weaving with 'stringy things' (5+)

Decorative ribbons, laces and wools make pretty weavings. With older children, you can also use thin wool and a darning needle to create a more traditional weaving.

You will need

• Stiff card
• Scissors
• String
• Sticky tape
• A selection of decorative ribbons, laces, silk cords
• Different coloured wool
• Darning needle

What to do

Decorative ribbon weaving: this activity is very similar to weaving with strips of fabric (*see Fabric weaving, page 123*), except that you use decorative laces and ribbons, rather than fabric. Make up a weaving card (*see Fabric weaving*). Weave lace, ribbons and other pretty things in and out of the strings.

Wool weaving (7+): cut notches in the top and bottom of the card, approximately half a centimetre apart. Wind coloured wool around the card to make the 'warp' (the upright threads). Thread a length of wool onto a darning needle. Leaving an end of about 5cm trailing from the edge of the frame, weave the wool in and out of the warp to make the 'weft' (the cross threads). Start at the top of the card and work from right to left. When you get to the end of the row, weave back through the warp, going from left to right. Work your way down the card, gently pushing each weft row upwards to keep the weaving tight. Start a new length of wool as you run out. When the whole card is finished, weave in the loose ends at the top and bottom of the card. As long as the

weaving is nice and tight, you can cut the warp threads at the top and bottom of the card to release the weaving.

> **Tip**
>
> *Once children get the hang of card weaving, they can experiment with different colours and patterns. Try weaving two or three rows in alternate colours. Choose contrasting colours for the warp threads to create a checked pattern.*

A weaving patchwork: pin or sew lots of different weavings to a large piece of sturdy fabric to make a patchwork wall hanging.

Collage person: glue a rectangular weaving to a sheet of stiff card and add a head, legs and arms cut from coloured card. Add woollen hair, ribbons, large brightly coloured buttons and shoes cut from brown felt.

Threading cards (3+)

Children can make their own threading cards by cutting out shapes and punching them with a hole puncher.

You will need

- Coloured card (choose the stiffest card that the children can cut)
- Scissors
- A hole puncher
- Brightly coloured silk cord, lace or wool
- Clear sticky tape
- Sequins, stickers, felt-tipped pens, gold and silver pens, glitter glue, PVA glue (optional)

What to do

Draw a large shape on the card. Younger children can draw a random shape, older children can draw the shape of a favourite object such as a car, a teddy bear or an animal. Encourage the children to keep the shapes simple. Cut out the shapes and punch round the edges with a hole puncher.

Tape one end of the thread to the back of the card and weave it in and out of the punched holes. When the threading is finished, tape the other end to the back of the card so that it is held securely. Decorate the card with felt-tipped pens, gold and silver stickers, sequins and blobs of glitter glue.

Use for

Christmas decorations: make a threading card using a star, Christmas tree or angel shape. Thread with gold or silver cord and decorate with gold and silver glitter and sticky stars. Tie a loop of cord through one of the holes so that the card can be hung up.

Valentine's and Mother's Day cards: make a threading card using a red heart or flower shape.
Thread with pink cord or embroidery silk and decorate with bits of lace and gold sequins.

Winding cards (4+)

Winding card made with white and red cotton and gold thread

As a variation on threading, try winding the thread around a card shape, rather than in
and out of the punched holes.

You will need

- Coloured card (choose the stiffest card that you can cut)
- Scissors
- Brightly coloured embroidery silk or thin wool
- Clear sticky tape
- Sequins, stickers, felt-tipped pens, gold and silver pens, glitter glue, PVA glue (optional)

What to do

Draw a simple shape such as circles, triangles, ovals and rectangles on the card. Cut
out the shape and make small, triangular notches around the edge. If you place the
notches opposite each other, you will end up with a regular pattern of thread. If you
place them randomly, you will end up with an irregular pattern. Both approaches are very
effective. You can also try cutting a window into the centre of the shape.

Tape one end of the thread to the back of the card. Wind the thread around the card, using the notches to hold it secure. When the winding is finished, tape the other end to the back of the card so that it is held securely. Decorate the card with felt-tipped pens, gold and silver stickers, sequins and blobs of glitter glue.

Use for

Mobiles: make lots of winding cards, using geometric shapes. Punch a hole in the top of each shape and thread through a loop of embroidery silk. Tie the decorated shapes to a ribbon covered wire coat hanger to make a mobile.

Christmas decorations: a green card triangular tree makes a good shape for a winding card. Use gold thread and decorate with sequins and glitter glue. Turn the card tree into a hanging decoration by adding an embroidery silk loop.

Dream catchers (5+)

A dream catcher is a traditional American Indian artefact. If you hang your dream catcher in the bedroom window, it is said to stop the good dreams from escaping. Use the 'winding' technique (see above) to make your own dream catcher.

You will need

- Stiff card
- A pair of compasses for drawing circles
- Scissors
- Holograph or shiny gift tape
- Embroidery silk
- About 50cm of thin ribbon
- 14 beads
- 6 small coloured feathers (available from craft shops or schools suppliers)
- PVA glue

What to do

Using the compasses, draw a circle on the stiff card, with a diameter of about 12cm. Create a ring by drawing a second circle inside the first circle, with a diameter of approximately 11cm.

Cut out the card ring.
Cut eight small nicks at evenly spaced points around the outer edge of the ring.
Twist short strips of gift tape around the ring, making sure that the nicks are not covered by the tape.

Tie a length of embroidery silk to one of the nicks, leaving an end of about 8cm.
Wind the silk across the ring, using the nicks to hold the silk secure and working around the ring to make a regular pattern.

Each time you wind the silk across the ring, thread on a bead.

Thread the silk twice through the bead to hold it secure.

When you reach the last nick, knot the silk around the ring.

Cut the ribbon into three similar lengths.

Thread two or three beads onto each of the ribbons and tie knots in the ends to hold the beads secure.

Push the ends of two feathers up into the bottom beads.

Tie the ribbons to the bottom of the ring so that they are evenly spaced out (if they slip, secure them with a blob of PVA glue).

Tie the loose end of silk into a loop and hang the dream catcher from the bedroom window.

Making threading and winding cards

It is essential that you use stiff card for all of these activities, particularly winding cards and dream catchers. If the card is too thin, it will bend out of shape when it is used. Test your card before giving it to the children. If the card is too stiff for them to cut, do the cutting for them.

Woollen pompoms (5+)

Woollen pompoms are great fun to make and they can be used in lots of different ways to brighten up a collage or model.

You will need

- Card
- A pair of compasses (for drawing circles)
- Scissors
- Wool

What to do

Using the compasses, draw two identical circles on the card.

Draw two smaller circles inside the larger circles to make thick rings.

Cut out the rings (don't worry if the cutting is a bit rough – the rings will be hidden by the wool.)

Fabric and buttons, wool and string

Place the two rings together and wind wool through the middle and around the rings.

When the wool nearly fills the central hole, cut through the strands by sliding the scissors in between the two layers of card.

When you have cut all the way round the circle, pull the two rings apart and tie a piece of wool firmly round the middle of the wool.

Remove the card rings and fluff out the pompom.

Tip
Experiment with combinations of different coloured wool.

Use for

Easter chicks: make small pompoms from yellow wool. Cut out a small diamond from orange card and fold it in half. Punch out two circles from black card with a hole puncher. Using PVA glue, stick the folded diamond and the circles onto the pompom, to represent the eyes and the beak. Wash out half an eggshell and glue the chick inside. Cut out a small card base for the eggshell and sponge paint it with green paint. The chick can also be used to decorate an Easter twig tree (*see Twig trees / An Easter tree, page 154*).

Snowmen: make a large white pompom for a snowman's body and a smaller pompom for the head. Glue the pompoms to a card background and stick on cut-out card features. Use real twigs for the arms. Add cotton wool, white tissue snow and white paper lace snowflakes (*see Paper cutting / Paper lace, page 78*).

Decorating clowns: make brightly coloured pompoms to decorate a collage clown. Stick the pompoms onto his hat and clothes, and use a bright red pompom for his nose. For a Pierrot type clown, stick black wool pompoms onto a white outfit.

Collage clothes: use pompoms to decorate bobble hats, dresses and coats.

Chapter 9

Sand and shells, stone, wood and glass

About sand and shells

Sand is a natural material that can be used for adding texture to many different kinds of artwork. You can gather small quantities from the beach or use sand from the sand box. Ready bought play sand has the advantage of being sterilised. This makes it the safest choice for playgroups and schools. Apart from sprinkling sand onto glue to make a collage, it can also be mixed with paint or clay to add an interesting grainy effect to landscapes, buildings and animals.

As an alternative, you can buy coloured sand from art and craft shops and schools suppliers. This can be used in the same way as glitter, although it has more of a glow than a sparkle – particularly if you use it on black card. Another way of using sand is to cut sandpaper into shapes and stick them onto a card background. Look out for different grades and colours of sandpaper, to add variety to your sandy pictures.

Like sand, shells can be collected from the beach or purchased from schools suppliers and craft shops. It is also possible to buy polished shells from seaside shops. Although they are a little more expensive, the polishing process gives a lovely glossy surface and brings out the colours and patterns of the shell. Use them as the centrepiece for a special picture, or turn them into shell models (*see Shell animals, page 145*).

About stone

Stone has many uses in art and craft. Rocks and pebbles with smooth surfaces can be painted. Different shapes, colours and sizes of stone can be piled up to make sculptures. Small pebbles can be stuck onto collages or pressed into Plasticine to make plaques, while gravel and shingle can be sprinkled onto a thick layer of glue.

Stones and pebbles are easy to find. Look out for interesting shapes and colours during walks on the beach or in the countryside. The best place to find gravel is the pet shop, where it is sold for fish tanks. Give it a good rinse before using it to add an authentic touch to landscapes or buildings. Always try to find stones and pebbles to suit a particular project. Pebbles for painting need to have a smooth surface, and they should also be flat bottomed so that they don't wobble. If you want to make stone sculptures, look out for thin, flat stones that are easy to pile up and stick.

A note of caution

Before gathering shells, sand, shingle and pebbles from coastal areas and the countryside, check that you are not contravening any bye-laws. Some beaches protect their environment by banning the removal of any natural items.

About wood

Wood gives endless choices, from twigs, bark and driftwood to slices of kindling or processed wood. Look out for wooden boxes, spoons and eggcups to decorate. Use spent matchsticks for collage and printing and turn off-cuts of wooden dowelling and wooden beams into models and constructions. As with so many art and craft scrap materials, it is useful to start a collection. Set up a 'wood box' and look out for scraps of wood and wooden items that may have a use in artwork.

Wood safety

Although wood is generally safe to use with children, always check for splinters or ragged edges. Use sandpaper to smooth surfaces and tear off any sharp, pointed twigs.

About glass

Glass makes an interesting and unusual surface for painting. You can either paint directly onto a window or use specialised glass paints to decorate drinking glasses and jam jars. Some schools suppliers and craft shops also sell perspex tiles and acetate sheets that can be painted and turned into window decals.

For painting on windows, you can use ordinary ready mixed or powder paint (*see Window painting, page 156 for more details*). If you want to create a lasting pattern on a glass item, you will need to use a special glass painting kit. Some schools suppliers also sell glass paints that can be peeled or wiped off after use.

Use sand in art to ...

• Add texture to collage
• Add texture to paint
• Add texture to clay

Use shells in art to ...

• Make hangings
• Make animal models
• Make painted plaster casts

Use stone in art to ...

• Make sculptures
• Make painted paperweights
• Make painted doorstops

Use wood in art to ...

• Make model trees
• Make monsters
• Make matchstick prints

Activities

Sand drawings (all ages)

Drawing in sand is an activity for all age groups. You can have impromptu drawing sessions in the sand box or on the beach, or you can provide sand trays for special sand drawing activities.

You will need

• Sand
• A sand box or sand pit
• A plain, shallow tray
• Shells, pebbles, twigs, leaves and other items (optional)
• Water
• Chopsticks or thick pencils

What to do

Work at the edge of the sand box, where the layer of sand is more likely to be thin.

Using a finger, draw patterns in the sand so that the base of the box shows through. If the layer of sand is too deep, add just a bit of water so that it will 'hold' the marks. Give the children a chopstick or thick pencil to draw with.

Sprinkle enough sand into the tray to cover the base. Leave the children to draw marks, patterns and pictures with their fingers. If a child wants to start afresh, gently shake the tray to make the sand smooth again. Introduce shells, feathers and other items to add to the pictures. Mix the sand with water and give children a chopstick or thick pencil to draw with. Do they prefer drawing on dry sand or wet sand?

Find a part of the beach where the sand is still wet and encourage the children to draw big pictures with a stick or a spade. Find shells, pebbles, seaweed and driftwood to decorate the picture.

> **Tip**
> *Mix different substances with the sand in the sand tray. Try oatmeal, lavender flowers, coloured sand, rice, lentils.*

Use for

Patterns: make rows of different lines in the sand – zig-zags, wavy lines, criss-crosses. Add rows of shells and small pebbles.

Sand creatures: make drawings of rock pool creatures such as crabs, sea snails and sea anemones. Add shells and seaweed to the drawing.

Sand castle drawings: make drawings of sand castles. Decorate with small pebbles and stones to add texture to the 'walls' of the castle and make brightly coloured flags to lay on the drawing.

Photographing sand drawings

Because sand drawings are not permanent the children can focus on enjoying the process, rather than worrying about the outcome. If you do want to record the end results, take photographs and mount them on card decorated with sand (*see below*) or sandy paint.

Sand collage (4+)

Sand can be sprinkled onto glue to add a natural, grainy texture to collage pictures. For a brighter effect, try using coloured sand on black card.

You will need

- Sand
- Coloured sand
- Sandpaper
- PVA glue
- Stiff card

What to do

Plain sand: spread glue onto a card background and sprinkle on the sand. Shake the excess sand onto newspaper. You can either spread out the glue to cover an area of card or dribble it from a bottle to make lines and shapes.

Coloured sand: use just one colour at a time and shake off the excess sand before going on to use another colour. You can also make your own coloured sand by adding dry powder paint to plain sand (wear overalls and have hand washing facilities nearby as this is quite a messy activity!).

Sandpaper: cut up bits of sandpaper and add them to a collage. You will need strong scissors as the sandpaper is quite tough. If necessary, cut out the shapes for the children. Look out for different grades and colours of sandpaper.

Use for

Buildings: sand and other substances such as oatmeal add an authentic stone-like quality to collage pictures of buildings.

Sandy beaches: sand collage makes the perfect 'sandy beach' background for seaside pictures.

Diwali sand pictures: celebrate Diwali by making traditional coloured sand pictures. Draw a pattern with a pencil, cover it with glue and sprinkle on the coloured sand.

Sand collage with the under threes

Even the youngest children can make sand collage pictures. Check that the glue flows easily and help them to hold and squeeze the bottle so that the glue dribbles out. See GLUING SAND AND GLITTER box *(page 144)* for more on using sand with little ones.

Sand sculptures (3+)

Damp sand makes a great modelling material. As with sand drawings the results are not permanent, leaving everyone free to enjoy the process rather than having to concentrate on the end result.

You will need

- Damp sand
- Small spades and table spoons
- Small rakes, chopsticks, wooden spoons and other 'mark making' implements
- Moulds such as small buckets, empty yoghurt pots, plastic chocolate box trays, jelly moulds, biscuit cutters, specialised sand and playdough moulds
- Items to decorate the sculptures, such as shells, pebbles, twigs, flags
- Clay (optional)
- A large sheet of stiff card cut from a cardboard packing case, or a wooden board

What to do

There are various ways to sculpt sand. Work in a sand pit or place a large sheet of stiff card or wood on the floor. As a starting point, introduce some of the following techniques and then leave the children to explore the sand in their own way:

Sand moulds: use a table spoon to fill a mould with damp sand, making sure that the sand is as densely packed as possible. Carefully turn the mould over and tap gently until it releases its contents.

Sculpting with hands: mould the damp sand into bumps, hills, towers, snakes and other shapes. Smooth over the surface of the sand with the fingers.

Patterns: use rakes, the handles of wooden spoons and chopsticks to make line patterns in the damp sand. Carefully press a finger into the sides of moulded shapes to make holes.

Decorating the sand: carefully press shells, twigs and other items into the damp sand. Arrange groups of pebbles, stones and shells around the base of sand castles and hills.

Sandy clay: mix sand with clay and use the clay to add details to a sand sculpture (*see pages 159 to 166 for more on clay modelling*).

Use for

Sand castles: make a traditional 'sand castle' using bucket moulds. Sculpt the walls from damp sand and decorate the castle with pebbles, gravel and flags. Add model knights on horse back.

Seashore displays: fill a large tray with damp sand and mould the sand into dunes and rock pools. Use the sandy setting to display seashells, seaweed, driftwood and other beach finds.

Some more 'sprinkly things'

There are lots of other grainy substances that can be sprinkled onto glue or mixed in with paint to create a texture. Try the following:

• oatmeal • lavender flowers • rice • lentils • millet • bulgar wheat
• small seeds such as sesame, mustard and alfalfa seeds
• puffed rice and crunched up cornflakes • dried herbs • glitter
• glass 'seed' beads (for older ones, due to choking hazard)
• sawdust (for older ones) • pine needles (for older ones)

Sandy paint (all ages)

Mixing sand and other substances with paint is a simple way to create an interesting new texture.

You will need

- Ready mixed or powder paint
- Sand and other 'sprinkly things'
- A thick brush
- Containers for mixing up the sandy paint
- Card or sturdy paper

What to do

Mix the paint with the sand. Try different quantities of sand to achieve different effects. Brush the sandy paint onto sturdy paper or card. Experiment with other substances such as oatmeal and sawdust. If the added substances give the paint a satisfying texture, the mixture can be used as finger paint. Try oatmeal or lavender flower finger paint, but stick to a brush for paint mixed with pine needles or sawdust!

Use for

Townscapes: as with sand collage, sandy paint can be used to add a stone-like texture to buildings, roads and pavements.

Seascapes: make a sandy beach with yellow and light brown sandy paint.

Sea creatures: use sandy paint to add texture to turtles, starfish, crabs and other sea creatures.

Landscapes: use oatmeal mixed with brown and green paint to add texture to paintings of fields, hills and trees.

Gluing sand and glitter

Keeping control of sand, glitter and other sprinkly things can be quite challenging, particularly for younger children. Try the following techniques:

Fingers and thumbs: put the glitter in a small pot and use the finger and thumb to sprinkle glitter onto the glue. This technique is useful for adding small quantities to a picture.

Salt pots: put the glitter into an empty salt pot or specialised glitter shaker and sprinkle over the glue. Shake the excess glitter onto a sheet of scrap paper, fold the paper in half and pour the glitter back into the pot.

Glitter trays: sprinkle glitter over the base of a tray and spread glue over a piece of paper. Place the paper on top of the glitter, glue side down. Gently press the paper to ensure that all the glue comes into contact with the glitter. Lift up the paper and shake the excess back into the tray.

Glitter pens: glitter pens consist of tubes filled with a mixture of glue and glitter. Simply squeeze blobs and lines of glitter onto the paper. The glittery glue can then be left to dry as a blob or a line, or smudged with the finger to create flat areas of glitter. The glue does tend to clog up the pen quite quickly. Make sure the pen is flowing freely and, if necessary, help little ones to squeeze out the glittery glue.

Gluey shapes

For an easy way to make glue shapes, dip a playdough cutter into a flat container of PVA glue. Press the cutter onto the paper to leave a gluey outline and sprinkle glitter or sand over the shape.

Shell animals (4+)

Animals made using
polished shells, Plasticine and cloves

The shapes and natural colours of shells lend themselves to making models of animals.

You will need

- A variety of shells in different shapes and sizes, including limpet shells and spiral shells
- Stiff card (as a base)
- PVA glue
- Plasticine
- Embroidery silks or wool

What to do

Look closely at the shells and think which animals they remind you of. Use Plasticine to mould legs, heads and other features. If necessary, secure the Plasticine with small dabs of PVA glue. You can also glue smaller shells or tiny pebbles onto larger shells to make ears and eyes. Use plenty of PVA glue to make sure the items are securely fixed. Glue the animal to a small base of stiff card. Spread the card with more glue and sprinkle on sand and gravel.

Use for

Tortoises: limpet shells make good tortoises. Mould Plasticine legs and a head for the tortoise and press them underneath the shell so that they stick out.

Mice: choose small spiral shells to make the body of a mouse. Flatten two small balls of Plasticine to make ears and attach them to the shell with a blob of PVA glue. Use a permanent felt-tipped pen to make the eyes and glue a length of embroidery silk to the back of the mouse to make the tail.

Snails: choose shells with a curly spiral pattern. Roll out a Plasticine sausage to make the body of the snail and press the shell on top.

Shell hangings (4+)

Display your seaside finds by turning seashells into an attractive hanging.

You will need

- Small spiral shells
- Clay
- A length of embroidery silk or colourful wool
- Decorative beads
- Small coloured feathers (available from craft shops and schools suppliers)
- A thin knitting needle

What to do

Press lumps of clay into the opening of the shells so that a small amount of clay is sticking out of the shell.

Carefully push a thin knitting needle through the exposed clay to make a hole. When the clay is dry, thread a shell onto a length of embroidery silk.

Wind the thread twice through the hole so that the shell is held secure. Leave a tail of silk, about 8cm long.

Thread a large, decorative bead onto the silk, a couple of centimetres above the shell.

Double thread the bead so that it is held secure on the silk.

Double thread a second shell onto the silk, just above the bead.

Continue until all the shells and beads have been threaded.

Finish off with a bead and poke a couple of feathers up into the hole of the bead.

Tie the loose end of embroidery silk into a loop and dangle the hanging from a hook on the ceiling or wall.

Handmade beads for shell hangings

Although you can use ready-made beads for a shell hanging, it is more effective to make your own.

Shell casts (4+)

Casting shells with plaster of Paris is an easy way to make an accurate model of the shell. Once the plaster is dry, the cast can be painted using natural, shell-like colours or bright, primary colours.

You will need

- Shells with strong patterns
- Plasticine
- Plaster of Paris (available from art shops and schools suppliers)
- Ready mixed or acrylic paints
- Thin brushes

What to do

Making the mould: mould the Plasticine into slabs. Make an impression of the shell by pressing it into the Plasticine. Take care not to smudge the impression as you remove it from the Plasticine. Younger children may need help with the process of making the mould.

Making the cast: mix plaster of Paris with water to make the consistency of double cream (*see About plaster of Paris, page 158*). Pour the wet plaster into the Plasticine mould. Gently tap the Plasticine a few times to make sure the plaster has seeped into all the crevices of the mould. When the plaster is dry, peel off the Plasticine to reveal the cast of the shell.

Decorating the cast: challenge older children to mix up colours as close as to the original shell as possible. Using a thin brush, can they make an exact copy of the shell? As an alternative, paint the shells in bright primary colours and glue on small beads, sequins and glitter.

Tip

'Shallow' shells often work best for this activity. If a shell is tall or spiky, it can be difficult to press fully into the Plasticine and it may get stuck as you pull it out. If in doubt, have a try-out before making the casts with the children.

Use for

Beach scenes: display painted plaster seashells on a tray of sand, dried seaweed and driftwood.

Painting pebbles (all ages)

Any age group can have a go at painting a pebble and the finished result makes a great gift. Use ready mixed or acrylic paint and add a coat of varnish to bring out the colours of the paint.

Painted Pebble by Joe (2)

You will need

- Paper and felt-tipped pens (for planning designs)
- Smooth pebbles
- Ready mixed or acrylic paint
- Thin brushes
- Cotton buds
- Craft varnish (for adult use only)
- PVA glue
- Felt

What to do

Planning the design: draw the shape of the pebble on a piece of paper. Use thin felt-tipped pens to plan the design for the pebble. Remind the children to keep their designs simple (patterns tend to look more effective than pictures). For a large pebble, try rows of different brush effects (*see page 25*). On smaller pebbles, try different coloured spots, simple flowers or hearts. You can also make some interesting abstract patterns by dribbling, flicking or spraying paint across the surface of a large pebble (*see Dribbling and flicking paint, page 27 and Spraying paint, page 28*).

Painting the pebble: check that the surface of the pebble is clean and dry. If necessary, give it a scrub with washing up liquid and a nail brush. Paint the design onto the pebble. When the paint is dry, give the pebble a coat of craft varnish or a PVA glaze. Cut out a piece of felt and stick it to the underneath of the pebble with PVA glue.

Painting pebbles with under 5s: younger children tend to mix the colours to a muddy brown, particularly when working on a small pebble. To prevent this from happening, choose a large flat stone. Put the paint in shallow containers and provide a cotton bud for each colour. Get the children to dab splodges of colour onto the surface of the pebble, and discourage them from mixing the colours too vigorously.

Use for

Paperweights: choose pebbles that are stable when placed on a flat surface. Once the paint is dry, glaze the surface with PVA glue or craft varnish and add felt to the base of the pebble.

Doorstops: choose a large pebble. Check that it doesn't wobble and that it is heavy enough to hold a door open. Plan a bold, brightly coloured abstract pattern. If possible, glaze the pebble with craft varnish rather than PVA, as this will provide a tougher finish.

Ladybirds: make a ladybird by covering a small, oval shaped pebble with red paint. Use a cotton bud to dab on spots of black paint.

Aboriginal stones (7+): native Australian people decorated stones with sacred symbols and pictures of legendary heroes and animals. Have a look at pictures of Aboriginal artefacts and encourage older children to paint their own Aboriginal stones. Use natural, earthy colours such as terracotta, white and brown.

'Magic stones' (7+): children who enjoy fantasy play love to make magic stones. Paint small, smooth pebbles with runes and mystical symbols such as stars, pentagons and spirals.

Pebble sculptures (5+)

Pebbles and stones make interesting 'building blocks' for abstract sculpture. Look out for stones with attractive shapes, colours and textures.

You will need

- A variety of stones and pebbles
- Sand and gravel (optional)
- Stiff card or a wooden board (for the base of the sculpture)
- PVA glue
- Craft varnish (optional)
- Acrylic paint (optional)

What to do

Gather a collection of stones and pebbles. Look out for stones with flat bottoms and smooth pebbles that can be piled on top of each other. Look out also for a variety of different colours. Working on a base of stiff card or a wooden board, build the pebbles and stones into a sculpture. Start off with the largest stones to make a secure

foundation for the sculpture. Concentrate on balancing the pebbles and use lots of PVA glue to stick the stones together. When the sculpture is completed, spread glue on the card base and sprinkle on sand or gravel. You can either glaze your sculpture to bring out the colours of the stone, or leave it in its natural state. To create a different effect, you can also paint the stones with acrylic paint, either before or after you have built the sculpture.

Use for

Ancient stone circles (7+): have a look at pictures of ancient stone circles, such as the famous example at Stonehenge. Gather together some tall flat stones and build your own model of a stone circle.

Stone walls (7+): nimble fingered older children can use carefully chosen stones and pebbles to build walls. Start with larger stones to make a base and use lots of PVA glue to stick the stones together. Use the walls on model landscapes.

Chalking on stone (all ages)

Use ordinary chalk or large sticks of playground chalk to draw on outdoor walls, paving slabs, playgrounds and other large stone areas.

You will need

- Sticks of large playground chalk
- Flat stone areas where it is appropriate to chalk

What to do

Make sure that your stone 'canvas' is clean and swept free of dust. Think about the shape of the stone area you plan to decorate – a paving slab, a brick, the face of a large rock. Design a pattern to fit into the shape of the canvas. For example, a patchwork of patterns looks effective on a grid of paving slabs. Outdoor chalking is a pleasant activity for a warm, sunny day but you can also make chalk drawings following a shower of rain. Crush some chalk ends and sprinkle them onto the wet surface (*see Powdered chalk / Chalk dust on wet paper, page 59*). Ask children to guess what happens to the chalk as it dries out and when it starts to rain again.

Use for

Nature record: make pictures to reflect the surroundings. Challenge the children to draw the different trees, flowers and birds that they see around them.

Weather record: designate an outdoor area as a weather record. Chalk little pictures of clouds, raindrops, suns and other symbols to reflect the day's weather.

Prehistoric cave drawings: with older children, study pictures of prehistoric cave drawings and make your own cave drawings on outdoor stone surfaces. Use charcoal as well as chalks.

Outdoor chalking – graffiti?

If you introduce outdoor chalking to children, you need to be very clear about where it is appropriate to draw. Help them to realise that chalking anywhere other than designated areas is graffiti!

Decorating wooden spoons (3+)

Wooden spoons make a cheap and useful resource for art and craft. They can be painted and decorated with shells, dried flowers and other bits and pieces, or turned into simple puppets.

You will need

- Wooden spoons
- Ready mixed or acrylic paint
- Thick and thin paint brushes
- Craft varnish
- PVA glue
- Decorative items such as dried flowers, small shells, small pebbles or beads
- Scissors
- Thin ribbon
- Wool
- Stiff card
- Scraps of fabric (optional)

Hanging Spoon by Sarah (4)

What to do

Decorated spoons: decorate the spoons with ready mixed paint. Older children can use a thin brush to paint patterns; younger children can use a large brush to cover the spoon with dabs of colour. When the paint is dry, give the spoon a coat of craft varnish or a PVA glaze. Pour a layer of PVA glue into the bowl of the spoon and arrange shells, dried flowers or beads on the glue. Leave to dry. Tie the ribbon in a bow around the handle of the spoon and tie the ends of the ribbon into a loop. Make sure the ribbon is securely attached to the handle by adding a blob of glue. Use the loop to hang up the spoon.

Spoon puppets: paint a face on the bowl of the spoon and add a coat of varnish or PVA glaze. When the varnish is dry, glue on wool to make hair. Cut out the shape of a body from stiff card. Paint the body or decorate with fabric and glue to the handle of the spoon. Leave some of the handle sticking out from beneath the body so that the children can hold the puppet.

Painting wooden things

There are lots of plain wooden items that can be painted and decorated with dried flowers, shells, sequins and other bits and pieces. Look out for the following:

- wooden egg cups • wooden napkin rings • wooden boxes
- wooden spatulas • 'slices' of smooth wood cut from a tree
- off-cuts of wooden dowelling, planed wooden beams and wooden boards

As with wooden spoons, use ready mixed or acrylic paint and bring out the colours of the paint with a coat of varnish.

Matchstick block printing (5+)

Spent matchsticks can be cut into different lengths and arranged on a wood block to make some interesting prints.

You will need

- Matchsticks
- A sharp knife (for adult use only)
- Wooden printing blocks (see Card printing blocks, page 65)
- PVA glue
- Ready mixed paint
- A medium sized brush
- Sugar paper for printing

What to do

Cut the matchsticks into different lengths. Spread a thick layer of PVA glue over the surface of the wooden block and stick on the matchsticks to make different patterns.

Try the following:

- A simple star shape
- A stick figure shape (use half a carrot to print a round head)
- Squares, rectangles, triangles, trapeziums
- Capital letters

What other patterns can you and your children come up with?

Use for

Christmas stars: make a matchstick printing block in the shape of a star. Mix yellow paint with PVA glue and use the star to make gift tags and Christmas cards. Print directly onto tissue paper to make wrapping paper. Sprinkle glitter on the prints and leave to dry.

Decorative borders: make matchstick printing blocks with shapes such as triangles and rectangles. Use the prints to decorate the borders of mounting paper, frames and the pages of home-made books.

Toilet signs: make two large stick figure printing blocks, one for 'ladies' and one for 'men'. Use the blocks to print signs for the toilet door.

Personalised cards: make printing blocks with initials and use them to make personalised greetings cards. Print the recipient's initials in the centre of the card and surround it with a decorative border.

'Signatures': use printing block initials to print a special 'signature' on a painting.

Wood sculptures (4+)

Wood comes in many different shapes, sizes and forms. Gather together different bits of wood and build them into an interesting sculpture.

You will need

- Scrap pieces of wood, such as off-cuts from beams, planks and dowelling, wooden board, twigs, chunks of tree, bark, driftwood, pine cones, lolly sticks, used matchsticks
- Sawdust (optional)
- A wooden board or stiff card base
- PVA glue
- Plasticine

Wood Collage by Rachel (11)

What to do

Working on a card or board base, build the wood bits into a sculpture. Start off with larger pieces of wood to make a foundation and use lots of PVA to stick the pieces together. Awkward shapes such as twigs can be attached using lumps of Plasticine. When the model is complete, spread glue over the base and sprinkle on sawdust.

Use for

An abstract sculpture: make an abstract sculpture to show off the colours, textures and shapes of the wood.

Monsters: make a wooden monster. Use the strange shapes of driftwood for the body and twigs to make talons or tentacles. Add Plasticine features such as green bulging eyes and red spiky teeth.

Twig trees (3+)

Plant a collection of twigs in a flower pot to make a 'tree'. Dress the tree with hanging decorations or lengths of ribbon, lace and wool.

You will need

- A variety of twigs
- A terracotta flower pot
- Plaster of Paris, clay or Plasticine
- Items for decorating the twigs (*see Use for section for ideas*)

What to do

Fill the flower pot with clay, Plasticine or plaster of Paris and press in the twigs. If you are using plaster, mix it up to the consistency of thick cream and hold the twigs in place until the plaster has set (it should set very quickly). Decorate the twigs in whatever way you wish.

Use for

A Christmas tree: spread a thin layer of PVA glue on some of the twigs and sprinkle on silver glitter. Hang small Christmas decorations from the twigs.

An Easter tree: hang small egg shell baskets from the twigs to make an Easter tree. Wash out some half egg shells. Glue thin ribbon around the bottom of the eggs and tie the loose ends into a bow. Hang the egg shell baskets from the twigs and fill with small flowers, chocolate eggs and chicks made from yellow pompoms (*see Woollen pompoms, page 136*).

Seasonal trees: make four twig trees. Turn one into a winter tree by gluing strands of cotton wool to the bare branches. Make the spring tree by gluing on white and pink tissue paper blossom (*see Tissue paper flowers, page 84*). Use cut-out green paper leaves for the summer tree and yellow, red and orange leaves for the autumn tree.

A 'stringy things' tree: wind wool, ribbon and other 'stringy things' around the twigs to make an abstract sculpture. (*see the MORE 'STRINGY THINGS' box on page 132 for further ideas*).

Making leaves for twig trees

Use a twig tree to show off your handmade leaves. Try the following:

- Cut-out wax rubbings of leaves
- Cut-out leaf prints
- Cut-out leaves decorated with spaghetti vein prints
- Pressed leaves
- Decorated pressed leaves
- Cut-out drawing of leaves
- Cut-out paintings of leaves

(*see page 113 for more ideas*)

Glass painting (5+)

Glass makes an interesting and different surface for painting. If you want your glass painting to be permanent, you will need to use specialised glass paint, available from art and craft shops and schools suppliers.

Painted glass pot

You will need

- White paper and felt-tipped pens for planning designs
- Glass or perspex surfaces
- Specialised glass paint
- Brushes

What to do

Choose a simple, repetitive design such as flowers, hearts or geometric shapes. Use felt-tipped pens and white paper to plan the design. Most glass painting sets include a tube of opaque grey or black paint for 'leading'. Encourage the children to give each shape in their designs a leaded outline. This makes the design stand out, as well as adding a professional looking finish.

Tip

Some glass paints can stand up to gentle washing, others are designed to be washed or peeled off the glass surface. If making glassware gifts, check that the paint is permanent.

Use for

Decorated glassware: use specialised glass paints to decorate plain drinking glasses. Choose a glass to suit a particular person and give it as a gift. Decorated jam jars can be turned into pen pots or containers for cotton wool balls, bath salts or home-made sweets.

Glass painting

Window painting (all ages)

You can use ordinary ready mixed or powder paint to paint directly onto windows. It washes off quite easily, as long as you don't leave it on for too long.

You will need

- Ready mixed or powder paint
- Brushes
- Newspaper

What to do

Start off by spreading newspaper onto the window sill and floor to protect against drips. Check that the window is clean and then let the children loose with their paint brushes. When you want to remove the paint, wash it off with a sponge and soapy water.

Tip

The longer you leave ready mixed or powder paint on a window, the harder it is to wash off. If you mix a little washing up liquid in with the paint, it will come off more easily. As an alternative, look out for washable glass paint – available from some schools suppliers.

Use for

Weather scenes: window painting is fun for weather scenes such as a big sun, a rainbow, a thunder storm with grey clouds and zig-zag lightning, or falling snow. Get the children to think about how the scenery outside the window provides a backdrop for their painting.

Stained glass windows: have a look at some stained glass windows with older children and encourage them to design and paint their own versions on a window pane.

Glass nuggets

Small glass nuggets make a very useful art and craft resource. They come in a wide range of jewel-like colours and their flat bottoms make them easy to glue onto a surface, as long as you use plenty of PVA glue. Use them to decorate box lids, cardboard crowns, papier mâché, wooden items and collage pictures.

Glass safety

Supervise children closely when they are painting on glass. Give younger children thick sided jam jars or acetate sheets to work on. Always work over a folded towel so that the glass is less likely to break if it is dropped.

Chapter 10

Clay and plaster of Paris and other modelling materials

About clay

Clay is a natural substance with a smooth, malleable texture. Used throughout history as a modelling material, it can be fashioned into pots, crockery, tiles or sculptures. Clay models can be left to harden naturally or fired in a kiln to achieve a tough, waterproof finish. If you are not using a kiln, look out for a type of clay called Newclay. This has tiny fibres worked into it, which prevent the clay from cracking as it dries out. Most clays are grey, but you can also buy terracotta to give a rich dark red colour to your models. Clay is easily available from art

and craft shops and schools suppliers. If you live in a clay area, you can experiment with digging up your own. It won't give such a fine finish to your models, but children love working with natural materials that they have sourced for themselves.

Clay is easy to decorate, and you don't need any specialist tools or materials. While it is still wet, you can make markings with anything from a knitting needle to a glue spatula. Once it has dried, you can paint it with ordinary ready mixed paint or acrylics, and glaze it with craft varnish or PVA glue. You can also use clay as a collage background by pressing in items while it is still wet or gluing on items once the surface has dried (*for more details about decorating clay, see the box on page 162*).

About plaster of Paris

Plaster of Paris comes in the form of a white powder which is then mixed with water to the consistency of cream. It differs from clay in that it is poured into a mould, rather than used for hands-on sculpting. It hardens quite quickly and the resulting models have a smooth, white surface that can be painted and decorated. Plaster of Paris is cheap and easily available from specialist art shops and schools suppliers. A little goes a long way, so a bag should last for quite a while.

Activities

Playing with clay

Let children play freely with clay, playdough and other modelling materials. For younger children, this helps them to discover the properties of the different materials. For older ones, it gives free range to their imaginations. Playing with modelling materials is also very therapeutic for unsettled or angry children. Provide tools such as biscuit cutters and plastic knives and see what they come up with.

Rolling sausages and snakes (4+)

The clay 'sausage' and its thinner cousin, the 'snake' are basic shapes that can be used in many different ways.

You will need

- Clay
- A board or table top with a wipeable surface
- A teaspoon
- A damp sponge in a saucer

What to do

Give the children a lump of clay. Roll the lump between the hands to lengthen the shape and then place it on the board and roll evenly to form a fat sausage. Challenge older children to roll their sausage into a snake. Roll evenly and slowly with a gentle pressure to prevent the snake from breaking. If the snake or sausage gets dry and cracked, dampen the fingers on the sponge and smooth over the surface of the clay.

Use for

Coil Pot by Rachel (10) and Jack (6)

Snails: roll a sausage and press a real spiral shell on top to make a snail.

Snakes: roll out a snake and form it into a coil or curvy snake-like shape. Paint the snake with bright colours and add a forked tongue cut from red card.

Coil pots: this is an activity for nimble fingered older children. Roll lots of snakes and make a base for your pot from a smooth plaque of clay (*see Rolling a pancake, page 161*). Press the end of one of the snakes to the

edge of the base and coil the snake around the base to build up the sides of the pot. Add new snakes as you run out. When the pot is finished, use a teaspoon to smooth over the coils on the inside of the pot (this strengthens the bond between the coils).

Rolling a ball (4+)

Like the sausage and the snake, a ball is the basis for many clay models.

You will need

- Clay
- A board or table top with a wipeable surface
- A damp sponge in a saucer

What to do

Roll a lump of clay into a ball between the hands. Get older ones to experiment with rolling the ball on the board. Which do they find easier? Try different pressures. Can they roll the ball into an egg shape? Press the ball into a fat disc using the palm of the hand. Dampen the fingers on the sponge and smooth over the surface.

Use for

Thumb Pot by Rachel (10) and Jack (6)

Thumb pots: dig a thumb into the centre of a clay ball and squeeze the edges to form a pot. Little ones can make a simple, thick sided pot. Older ones can squeeze until the edges of the pot are thin and delicate. Experiment with different styles:

- make a thick flat rim that can be decorated with marks
- pinch the rim until it is as thin as paper
- press gently down on the rim to fold it over
- make a wide pot so that you can decorate the base on the inside

Don't forget to smooth out any cracks with wet fingers.

Animals: roll a ball of clay and then pinch out the legs, ears and tail to create an animal. This technique makes for a sturdier model as the limbs do not have to be made separately and then joined onto the body. Add on markings, eyes and other details (*see the DECORATING CLAY/ GARLIC PRESSES box, page 163*). When the clay has dried, paint and glaze the animal.

Beads: roll small clay balls and gently skewer a thin knitting needle through the centre. Leave the beads to dry and then paint and glaze them before stringing them on a ribbon or leather thong.

Clay and plaster of Paris and other modelling materials

Snowmen: roll two balls of clay, one a little smaller than the other and place the smaller ball on top of the larger to make the snowman's head and body. Stick two twigs on either side of the snowman's body. When the clay has dried, paint the balls with several coats of white paint. Roll some tiny balls and paint them black to represent coal. Glue them on to represent the snowman's face and buttons. Roll a small sausage of clay and carefully slice off the two ends to create a cylinder (use a sharp knife so that the cutting doesn't squash the cylinder – adults only). Squash a small ball to make a disc and attach it to the cylinder to make a hat. Press the hat against the snowman's head so that it takes on the shape of the head and leave it to dry. Paint the hat brown and then stick it to the head with lots of PVA glue. Finish off the snowman by gluing a strip of colourful fabric around his neck to make a scarf.

Candle holders: roll a ball of clay and press a candle into the top of the clay. Flatten the base of the ball slightly so that the holder will stand up. While the clay is still wet, decorate the candle holder with markings or leave to dry and add a coat of paint. If you are making Christmas candles, tie a Christmassy ribbon around the body of the candle holder and stick on some glitter.

Candle Holder by Rachel (10) and Jack (6)

Rolling a pancake (4+)

The smooth surface of a clay pancake is great for decorating with markings and it can be used as the base for plaques, boxes and other models.

You will need

- Clay
- A board or table top with a wipeable surface
- A rolling pin
- A damp, tightly woven cloth such as an old cotton handkerchief
- A damp sponge in a saucer
- A plastic knife / biscuit cutters

What to do

Roll a lump of clay into a rough ball and place it on the damp cloth. Using a rolling pin, roll the ball into a pancake. Smooth the surface of the clay with damp fingers to get rid of any cracks. Cut the pancake into the shape you want or use a biscuit cutter. Once your shape is finished, peel it carefully off the damp cloth and leave it on a board to dry.

Clay and plaster of Paris and other modelling materials

Use for

Decorative plaques: roll a pancake to the thickness of about 1cm and cut it into a square, rectangle or diamond. Use a biscuit cutter to make circular or oval shapes. Use different tools to make markings in the clay, or press items into the clay to make a pattern (see the DECORATING CLAY box below). Leave younger children to make random patterns and encourage older ones to work around basic shapes such as rows, concentric circles or stars. Finish off with paint and a glaze, or leave the clay in its natural state. Tape a loop of ribbon to the back of the plaque so that it can be hung on the wall.

Nature tiles: a clay tile makes a natural canvas for displaying nature finds; small pebbles and stones, fossils, shells, crystals, skeleton leaves, twigs and feathers can all be pressed into damp clay. When the clay has dried, lean the tile against a plate stand and display on the mantlepiece.

Slab boxes and houses: this is an activity for older children who can use a ruler. Roll out five pancakes, at least 3/4cm thick. Cut them into squares or rectangles, measuring them so that they fit together to make a base and four sides. Use water to dampen the edges and join the slabs to make a box. Check that the joins are well bonded together. If necessary, add strength by rolling out some thin snakes and pressing them firmly into the inside angles of the box. To make a house, cut windows and a door into the slabs before joining them together. Add markings to represent bricks and tiles.

Bases: clay pancakes make a good base for any kind of model. The base can be decorated with markings while the clay is still wet, or you can stick on small items once the clay has dried. Try sawdust for a wooden sculpture, glitter for a Christmassy model, straw for animals or gravel for a model house.

Decorating clay

Clay makes the perfect canvas for markings or painted patterns. You can also use clay as a collage background by sticking lots of interesting bits and pieces into the wet surface of your model, pot or plaque. Try the following:

- **Markings:** while the clay is still damp, make markings with tools such as glue spatulas, matchsticks, chopsticks, cocktail sticks (carefully supervised), knitting needles, pencils (both ends) and plastic drinking straws. Try dots, circles, nicks, zig-zags, wavy and straight lines.

- **Prints:** use a comb to scrape a pattern into the clay before it dries. Roll a pastry wheel or toy tractor across a damp clay surface. Press in items with a raised pattern to make a print in the clay; experiment with Lego bricks, Sticklebricks, metal sieves, cheese graters, wicker baskets, shells, loosely woven fabric such as hessian and coarse sandpaper.

- **Clay collage:** while the clay is still wet, press in beads, buttons, sequins, glass nuggets, crystals, shells, feathers, dried beans and pulses, seeds, twigs or dried flower heads. Bear in mind that clay shrinks as it dries. Check that your items are still held fast once the model is dry and secure any loose bits with a dab of PVA glue.

- **Painting and glazing:** paint the surface of hardened clay with ready mixed or acrylic paint. When the paint has dried, brush over with craft varnish (for adult use only). For a gentler glaze that the children can do by themselves, use a solution of PVA glue and water (approx two parts glue to one part water – don't worry, the glue will dry clear!).

- **Garlic presses:** put a small lump of clay inside an old garlic press and squeeze. Enjoy watching the tiny worms come wriggling out and then use them for hair, thatched roofs or vegetation.

Storing and preparing clay

Clay must be kept airtight, otherwise it will dry up. Wrap it in clingfilm and a plastic bag, and keep it in a sealed plastic box. If the clay has become a little hard to manipulate, wrap it in damp cloths for a while – the clay will absorb the moisture and it should become easier to work. To re-use bits and pieces, squash them into a rough ball. Using the heel of your hand, press the ball against a board to make a wedge. Keep turning the wedge and pressing until the pieces are bonded together. The action is the opposite from kneading bread – pressing out the air bubbles rather than folding them in. If you are preparing the clay to be fired in a kiln, you need to get rid of all the air bubbles or the model will explode when the clay is heated. You don't have to be so particular if the clay is drying naturally, although you should still ensure that there are no large holes or gaps. To check that you have a solid lump, slice through the clay with a cheese wire and have a look at the centre. A cheese wire is also the easiest way to slice chunks from a large piece of clay. To make your own cheese wire, separate a wooden clothes peg and tie a length of fishing line or a guitar string between the two halves.

Plaster of Paris models (3+)

Plaster of Paris can be poured into a mould to make a model. You can buy rubber moulds or use the following technique to make your own shapes.

You will need

- Plaster of Paris
- Biscuit cutters
- Plasticine
- A pot and spoon for mixing the plaster of Paris
- Ready mixed paint
- PVA glue

What to do

Flatten a piece of Plasticine to make a base and press a biscuit cutter into the Plasticine to form a watertight mould. Mix the plaster of Paris to the consistency of double cream and spoon it into the mould. When the plaster of Paris has set, peel off

the Plasticine base and push the plaster shape out of the mould. Decorate with paint.

Tip
Do a test by pouring a little plaster of Paris into your mould and leaving it to dry. If the plaster sticks, smear a thin layer of Vaseline around the interior of the biscuit cutter before using it for the finished item.

Use for

Paperweights: choose biscuit cutters to suit your project, for example a heart shape for Valentine's Day, a flower for Mother's Day or a Christmassy shape for a Christmas gift. Decorate the shape and stick felt onto the bottom to make a paperweight. If the plaster soaks up your paint and looks a bit dull, mix some PVA glue with the paint to give a stronger colour and glossy finish.

Hanging decorations: pour a thin layer of plaster into your mould. When dry, tape a loop of ribbon to the back to turn it into a hanging decoration.

Plaster of Paris bandages

Plaster of Paris bandages are available from some schools suppliers and large art and craft stores. Similar to the bandages used to make casts for broken limbs, they are useful for adding a smooth layer to models. Make a base from a substance such as chicken wire, soak the bandages in water and drape them over the base. Once they have dried, your model will have a smooth surface that can be painted or decorated with collage.

Plaster of Paris casts (4+)

With its liquid consistency and quick air-drying properties, plaster of Paris is perfect for making casts.

You will need

• Plaster of Paris
• Plasticine
• Small items with strong relief patterns, such as shells
• A pot and spoon for mixing the plaster of Paris

What to do

Mould the Plasticine into a thick slab. Carefully press an item into the Plasticine to make an impression. Gently ease out the item, taking care not to smudge the impression. Mix the plaster of Paris to the consistency of double cream and pour it into the Plasticine mould. When the plaster has dried, peel off the Plasticine to reveal your plaster cast.

Clay and plaster of Paris and other modelling materials

Use for

Model shells: use a thin brush to paint your shell casts the colour of real shells. Use them as ornaments or as part of a seaside model or collage.

Saltdough

Saltdough is easy to make at home. It is great for Christmas decorations, candle holders, picture frames and other models and sculptures that you want to keep.

Basic recipe

- 1 cup of salt
- 1 cup of water
- 2 cups of plain flour

Dissolve the salt in the water and then mix in the flour, little by little. Use the dough to make sculptures and models and then bake in the oven at 100°C (200°F or gas mark 1⁄4). The length of time needed will depend on the size and thickness of the dough. The model is done once it is hard and sounds hollow when tapped. If you want a brown finish, bake for longer. The dough can also be left for a couple of days to dry out, but it will not be so durable. Once it is cool, the models can be painted with ready mixed or acrylic paints, and varnished with PVA glue or craft varnish.

Variations

- Add a tablespoon of vegetable oil to make the dough easier to manipulate.
- Experiment with different flours, such as wholemeal or rye.
- Stir in more salt to get a granular effect.
- Colour the dough by kneading in food colouring.

Tip
Avoid storing saltdough decorations in a damp environment, such as a loft. Unless you have given the model a thorough coat of waterproof varnish, the dough will absorb the moisture and become soggy.

Playdough

Playdough is great for little ones who don't have strong enough hands for clay. It is easy to make at home.

Basic recipe

- 1⁄2 cup of salt
- 1 cup of water
- 1 cup of plain flour
- 2 tablespoons of cream of tartar
- 2 tablespoons of vegetable oil

Put all the ingredients in a large saucepan and stir over a moderate heat until the dough forms a lump. Leave to cool and then knead the playdough until smooth. Store in an airtight bag or tin.

Variations

- To make the dough smell nice, add a few drops of vanilla essence.
- Colour the dough by adding food colouring to the water before mixing it in.
- Make sparkly dough by adding gold or silver glitter.

Tip
The high salt content of playdough makes it potentially dangerous for animals. Keep it out of the way of pets, particularly dogs!

Index